OTHER BOOKS BY ALPHONSO PINKNEY

The Committed: White Activists in the Civil Rights Movement

Black Americans

Poverty and Politics in Harlem (with Roger Woock)

The American Way of Violence

Alphonso Pinkney

THE AMERICAN WAY OF VIOLENCE

RANDOM HOUSE

New York

 Published in the United States by Random House, Inc., New York, and simultaneously in Canada by Random House of Canada Limited, Toronto.

ISBN: 0-394-46173-8

Library of Congress Catalog Card Number: 71-174712

Manufactured in the United States of America by H. Wolff Book Manufacturing Co., N. Y.

98765432

FIRST EDITION

To the memory of the countless millions destroyed by American violence, especially Blacks, Indians, Indochinese and other Third World peoples

Violence is as American as cherry pie.

—H. RAP BROWN

Preface

In July 1967 a reporter from *Time* magazine asked me if I could agree with him that the most violent people in American society were young black males. This was at the time of the black uprising in Newark. When I suggested that on the contrary, young black men were more the victims of violence than its initiators, and that the real purveyors of violence in Newark were the police, National Guardsmen and state troopers who were slaughtering black people, he seemed bewildered. Like most Americans, this reporter regarded attacks on property such as arson and looting to be at least as grave violations of human rights as the destruction of human beings. Hence for blacks to destroy or damage property valued at $15 million was in many ways a more serious offense than the killing of 26 persons and the injuring of another 1,100 by those summoned to restore order.

One of the features of a materialistic society is a concomitant depreciation of human beings; in the United States, private property tends actually to be esteemed over human life. Because of this distorted ordering of priorities, much of the recent writing on the subject of violence emphasizes property destruction and minimizes the destruction of human beings. This book, concerned with the violation of persons, is an effort to correct the imbalance.

Violence, as a concept, is broad. It may be overt or subtle, individual or institutional. Overt acts of violence involve the destruction of human beings through the use of physical force. Subtle forms of violence, which are in many ways equally destructive of persons, cover a much broader range of human activity. They may be seen in such phenomena as hunger and malnutrition, inadequate medical care, substandard housing, unemployment and underemployment, inadequate and inferior education, and similar destructive conditions imposed on human beings. Subtle forms of violence are especially reprehensible when they occur on a wide scale in a society which is among the first in history with the resources to release its citizens from these privations.

Violence in addition consists of both individual and institutionalized acts of physical force against persons. Crimes of violence such as homicide, rape, and aggravated assault are most often individual acts, while such phenomena as warfare, police brutality, capital punishment and many other uses of force against nonwhite ethnic minorities, even by individuals, are institutionalized.

I have not attempted to present material on those features of American life which are good and noble; there is no dearth of accounts in praise of America. Even the National

Commission on the Causes and Prevention of Violence felt impelled to include a chapter in its final report in which a foreign newspaper correspondent was asked to appraise "the many strengths of America" in an effort "to view our institutions in full focus." If the omission of such a discussion renders the account presented here unbalanced, I make no apology. My concern is the violation of persons, without their consent, through the overt application of force against them.

My theme is that the United States is an unusually violent society, that such behavior has characterized this society both domestically and in its relations with other countries throughout its history, and that violence thrives in America because the social climate nurtures and rewards it. From the massacre of Indians and the enslavement of blacks in the early years of the nation's history, to the assault on the populations of Hiroshima and Nagasaki in the middle of the twentieth century, to the present-day slaughter of Indochinese peasants and members of the Black Panther Party, American society has clearly demonstrated its propensity for human destruction.

In spite of the pervasiveness of America's violence, the leaders of this country are obsessed with the minor defensive violence of black militants and the destruction of property by youthful citizens who resort to such acts in anguished attempts to force a reordering of national priorities and the affirmation of policies supportive of human life. Violence will continue to flourish in American society so long as citizens and the leaders they elect insist upon remaining oblivious to its real manifestations, concentrating instead on the relatively petty actions of those who themselves suffer from the society's brutality. More important, however, violence will continue to thrive so long as America's social institutions are organized around values which lead to the debasement of human beings. In such a climate individuals are systematically stripped of their humanity and acts of cruelty toward human beings abound.

The motivation for writing this book and many of the ideas contained in it were generated by my participation, over a period of more than five years, in a Columbia University seminar on Human Maladaptation in Modern Society. Throughout this period the seminar was devoted exclusively to a discussion of violence. In May of 1967, when I presented a paper on "Violence as a Theme in American Culture," many of the participants in the seminar were distressed by the ideas put forth. However, the black uprisings that summer and the political assassinations the following spring served to give credence to these ideas and to gain a measure of acceptance of them from the seminar's participants.

The Department of Sociology of the University of Chicago provided financial support and an agreeable atmosphere, both of which facilitated the preparation of this volume. David Sternberg generously agreed to read the manuscript, and presented many useful suggestions.

Contents

The American Way of Violence

I

►►►►►►

Introduction: On Violence in America

After the assassination of Robert F. Kennedy on June 4, 1968, the President of the United States addressed a nationwide radio and television audience on the shooting. Among other things, he announced the establishment of a commission of well-known Americans to study the phenomenon of violence in American society. The commission was charged with investigating "the causes, the occurrence and the control of physical violence across this nation, from assassination that is motivated by prejudice and by ideology, and by politics and by insanity; to violence in our city streets and even in our homes." He asked the members of the commission to address themselves to the following questions: "What in the nature of our people and the environment of our society makes possible such murder and such violence?" "How does it happen?" "What can be done to prevent assassinations?" "What can be done to further protect public figures?" "What can be done to eliminate the basic causes of these aberrations?"

The assassination of Senator Kennedy occurred approximately five years after that of NAACP official Medgar Evers in Mississippi, four and one-half years after the assassination of John F. Kennedy in Dallas, slightly more than three years after the assassination of Malcolm X in New York City, and two months after the assassination of Martin Luther King, Jr., in Memphis, Tennessee.

The 1960's were especially violent years. On July 14, 1966, eight student nurses were murdered in Chicago in the early morning hours, each young woman killed by stabbing and strangulation. A 24-year-old ex-convict and former merchant sailor, Richard Benjamin Speck, was charged with and later convicted of the crime.

Two weeks later, at high noon on August 1, a former Eagle Scout and ex-marine, Charles Joseph Whitman, climbed to the observation deck of a tower on the campus of the University of Texas at Austin. Armed with two rifles, a carbine, a shotgun and three pistols, he proceeded to kill 13 persons and an unborn baby and to wound 31 others.

In November of that year an 18-year-old high school senior, Robert Benjamin Smith, walked into a beauty college in Mesa, Arizona, forced seven women and children to lie on the floor and shot each twice in the head. Of the seven, only two survived. Smith killed his victims with a .22 caliber target pistol which had been given to him by his parents.

Also during 1966 five women, all over 50 years of age, were sexually assaulted and murdered in Cincinnati, Ohio. And in Milwaukee, Wisconsin, three young girls were brutally stabbed to death. In each of these cases, it was suspected that a single individual was responsible for the mass killings.

In addition, in the four-year period between 1965 and 1968 hundreds of persons were killed and thousands more injured during the black uprisings in Los Angeles, Cleveland, Newark, Detroit and some 200 other American cities in every region of the country.

In August 1968 the violence initiated by the police in response to protests at the Democratic National Convention in Chicago shocked many Americans, but many more took it in stride. They were accustomed, apparently, to behavior described as a "police riot" in the Walker Report, prepared by a study team of the National Commission on the Causes and Prevention of Violence. More than 1,000 people were injured in this eruption of violence.

As students at colleges and universities around the country demanded reforms in the educational system, they met violence at the hands of the police. At Columbia University more than 100 students, members of the faculty and staff were injured in April and May of 1968, when New York City policemen were summoned to the campus to eject students from buildings which they had occupied.

The following April a force of more than 400 helmeted state and local policemen swarmed onto the campus of Harvard University to remove more than 300 students from the administration building. Armed with night sticks, they charged into students massed on the steps of the building. Some 50 persons suffered injuries when they were kicked and beaten by the police.

In May 1969 one person was killed, one blinded and some 200 others injured when students at the University of California at Berkeley and local residents were attacked by local police, sheriff's deputies and National Guard troops. They were attempting to convert a vacant lot owned by the university into a public park for the use of all the people.

Throughout the second half of the 1960's, as a backdrop to this violence, millions of persons were killed or injured in Vietnam, including approximately 300,000 Americans, in one of the bloodiest and cruellest wars in human history.

In most of the larger cities of the country the rate of violent crime is so high that many citizens are afraid to walk the streets in their neighborhoods after nightfall. In the United States one violent crime (murder, forcible rape, robbery, assault) occurs every 54 seconds. The most serious of these crimes—murder—occurs at a rate of approximately one every half-hour. Most elected officials require extensive police protection from the people they are ostensibly representing when they appear in public. And with good reason: an American President, for example, is the target of an assassination attempt every 25 years—half of which have succeeded. In many other countries streets and public parks are safe at all times, and public officials at all levels appear among the citizenry unguarded. The Prime Minister of Sweden, for instance, travels between his home and office without protection on public transportation.

And in the face of all this, there persists in the United States the myth that Americans are a peaceful, nonviolent people. American history suggests the opposite. As a nation, the United States owes its existence to a violent revolution. Before that time the Europeans who colonized North America established their settlements by killing Indians and by a massive act of violence against black people. Throughout the 250 years of slavery, violence was the normal way of dealing with the black man. Continuous violence—both institutionalized and individual—has been an integral part of American life. Wars and murders have been and continue to be as characteristically American as virtually any other aspect of the culture.

The persistence of the myth of nonviolence in America makes almost hopeless the task of dealing with one of America's most serious social problems. It is within this mythical context that the President can refer to acts of violence in the United States as "aberrations." In 1965, when the black people in the Watts section of Los Angeles staged the first of a series of uprisings, the President called their behavior "shocking" and in a prepared statement on August 14 said: "I urge every person in a position of leadership to make every effort to restore order in Los Angeles. Killing, rioting and looting are contrary to the best traditions of this country." The following day he issued another statement in which he said, "There is no greater wrong, in our democracy, than violent, willful disregard of law." These were the words of a President who had not long before ordered the daily unprovoked bombing of North Vietnam, an act of violence virtually without precedent in human history, and directed a level of violence against the South Vietnamese people in "willful disregard" of international law which appears to many Americans to be only slightly less barbarous than the practices of the leaders of the Third Reich against Jews.

But is violent behavior endemic to the human condition? This question has plagued mankind for many centuries, and in recent years Robert Ardrey and Konrad Lorenz, among others, have revived the debate on whether mankind is innately aggressive. Both of them argue the affirmative. Many other scholars, however, present convincing evidence, often ignored by Ardrey and Lorenz, that aggressive and violent behavior, while prevalent, are not part of man's instinctive endowment; that it is not biologically determined, but in fact a cultural prescription.

The most compelling argument against the Ardrey-Lorenz position is the ethnographic data providing examples of human societies in which violent behavior is either totally or relatively absent. The Arapesh of New Guinea, the Lepchas of Sikkim, and the Pygmies of the Congo rain forest are all societies in which acts of violence do not occur. Similarly, while many other tribes of American Indians have histories of aggressive and war-like behavior, the Zuni Indians of the American Southwest are a peaceful people. Finally, the Eskimos are a people among whom warfare, even defensive warfare, is unknown. While they have always lived under adverse physical circumstances, they have never engaged in war, either among themselves or with outsiders. Moreover, these various peoples live in widely different physical environments. In some cases (that of the Pygmies, for example) the physical surroundings are not harsh, but in others (that of the Eskimos) life is extremely difficult.

Further, even among industrialized countries at the present time the incidence and types of violence vary from culture to culture. Sweden, one of the most industrialized of modern nation-states, has not been engaged in a war for more than a century and a half. And in addition to their strong aversion to engaging in warfare themselves, Swedes are extremely critical of warlike behavior on the part of other countries. The United States, on the other hand, is a country in which warfare (internal or external) has been a basic part of social organization and foreign policy since its inception as a nation-state. In the last century and a half the United States has been engaged in warfare somewhere in the world for all but a dozen or so years. And the people of the United States have often been eager to fight wars even when their government has been reluctant.

The violent crime rate also varies widely among the industrialized countries of the world. The homicide rate is a fairly reliable indicator of the level of violence in a country, and in 1967 the rate in industrialized countries varied anywhere from 5.6 per 100,000 population in the United States to 0.4 per 100,000 population in Ireland. Predictably, the homicide rate in the United States was more than twice that of any other industrialized nation.

Widespread acts of violence are not peculiar to the United States, however, for such acts have occurred and continue to occur in many other countries. Indeed, on the world scene, peace has been atypical and war has been normal. The twentieth century alone has witnessed two world wars, which have accounted for millions of deaths, and hundreds of localized wars, which have accounted for even more millions of deaths. Periods in which no country has been at war with another country have been rare in this century. Massive acts of violence abound. The Third Reich in Germany was responsible for the slaughter of millions of human beings. Each of the major European colonial powers has engaged in widespread acts of violence against the indigenous nonwhite peoples of Africa and Asia, most notably the Belgians in the Congo, the British in India, the Dutch in Indonesia, and the French in Algeria. In recent years, hundreds of thousands of Communists have been murdered in Indonesia. There have been frequent tribal slaughters in Africa, as among the Ibos, Hausas and Yorubas in Nigeria. And true social revolutions are usually accompanied by violence, as in the Soviet Union and the People's Republic of China.

Yet in no case would these acts have taken place if they had not been sanctioned by the societies in which they occurred, or by the society which committed them against another society. The individuals responsible for committing them learned such behavior from the culture in which they lived.

As for the United States, although it is hardly the only

violent society in the world, it is certainly one of the most violent. Furthermore, the American tradition of violence is a long-standing one: the outgrowth of historical forces which persist among its people. Calvinism, for instance, has played a crucial role in American history, with its affirmation of the doctrine of predestination and identification of divine election and worldly riches. A political consequence of the doctrine of predestination was that it led its followers to conclude that some people were meant by God to lead and others to follow, with whole groups of people categorized as either saved or doomed. This doctrine became associated with the notion of racial inferiority, justifying the enslavement of blacks and the extermination of Indians. Calvinists believed also that God bestowed his special blessings on those who dilligently sought worldly goods. In fact, according to R. H. Tawney, "Capitalism was the social counterpart of Calvinist theology." Profits were seen as proof of one's good works.

And Calvinist belief had another political consequence for society. It meant that those chosen by God could wage wars of destruction against all others, destined as these others were for hell. To wage war against those who were both damned and stood in the way of the profit motive was thus an act of highest service to God.

In the nineteenth century these ideas were reinforced by the spread of Social Darwinism. This theory of social evolution presupposed natural inequalities among people, based on the Darwinian thesis of natural selection, which held that only those forms of life survived which made successful adaptations to the dangers of the physical environment. Social Darwinism held that those less fit would either be eliminated or subordinated and therefore provided justification not only for differential access to social rewards but also for slavery and extermination.

The influence of Social Darwinism, like that of Calvinism, has diminshed in twentieth-century America, but both have left their mark on the American character.

In addition to its tradition of the use of force to maintain the profit system and its general lawlessness, cultural supports for violent behavior can be found throughout American society, facilitating, nurturing and rewarding such behavior. In short, these cultural factors assist in keeping the American tradition of violence alive.

There are so many contradictions and inconsistencies in American life that frustration is a constant state of affairs for large segments of the population. Such cultural ideals as monetary success, equality, freedom and democracy are mere myths which lose meaning in the face of widespread poverty and oppression. Violence frequently results from the frustration which individuals feel when they fail to satisfy legitimate aspirations. The society is generally an inhumane one.

The mass media, especially television, thrive on presenting steady doses of violence to eager viewers, listeners and readers. We live in one of the few countries in the modern world where one can possess virtually any type of deadly weapon for the expenditure of a relatively small sum of money. Attempts to control the sale of weapons through meaningful legislation have met with defeat, usually as a result of pressure from the National Rifle Association and other groups which maintain that such legislation would be a violation of American tradition and the Constitutional right of citizens to keep and bear arms. The Cold War climate of anti-Communism in the United States rewards "patriotic" acts of violence domestically and internationally. In large sectors of the population, patriots consider it their responsibility to attack anyone who disagrees with them. Whenever there is a peace parade or an anti-war demonstration, super-patriots can be expected to commit acts of violence against the demonstrators, often with the approval or direct assistance of the police. This violent atmosphere encourages further acts of violence by Americans against people the world over—for example, in Cuba, the Dominican Republic and Vietnam, to cite but a few of the recent examples.

In America violence against racial minorities has frequently been encouraged and has been viewed as somehow qualitatively different from acts of violence against white persons. The original colonies paid bounties for the scalps of Indians; public lynchings of blacks attracted thousands of gleeful spectators; white trigger-happy policemen still execute blacks on the slightest provocation, real or imagined, without public disapproval. And in recent years, white political dissenters have met the same acts of violence which had traditionally been reserved for racial minorities.

Finally, American society is characteristically unresponsive to reasoned criticism and demands for social change, forcing individuals and groups with legitimate grievances to seek to redress them through violent means. For hundreds of years black people have attempted to liberate themselves from oppression peacefully, but they have been constantly rebuffed. Now they have begun to feel that one way to achieve their legitimate goals is through rebellion, which generates still more violence on the part of their opponents. Similarly, the youth of the New Left are attempting to challenge many of the more anti-democratic and repressive features of the society. After many rebuffs they have turned to a policy of confrontation with the established order, and frequently to acts of terrorism.

That the United States is one of the most violent countries in the world, both domestically and in its relations with other countries, has finally received a measure of public recognition. Indeed, the reports of the National Commission on the Causes and Prevention of Violence stand as proof that future national character studies and social problems textbooks will not be able to ignore one of the most serious questions plaguing the country.

The war in Vietnam and the brutality which American forces have employed in destroying a people and their culture have horrified onlookers throughout the world as few other acts of violence have. The violence inflicted upon American citizens with enough humanity left to protest against the war and other injustices, as well as the alarmingly high violent crime rate and the increased recognition of America's bloody past, have led many Americans to agree with the remarks of Arthur Schlesinger, Jr., in a commencement address delivered the day after the assassination of Robert Kennedy: "The world today is asking a terrible question—a question which every citizen of this republic should be putting to himself: What sort of people are we, we Americans? The most frightening people on this planet."

I I

▶▶▶▶▶

The Prevalence of Violence

The present chapter presents a brief overview of American violence, concentrating on four areas: crimes of violence, war, labor-management relations, and child abuse. No attempt is made to present exhaustive studies in each of these areas; rather, the purpose is to illustrate the prevalance of violence in America through these four bloody examples.

Crimes of Violence

According to the National Commission on the Causes and Prevention of Violence, crimes of violence are so widespread in America that the United States is by far the most criminal nation in the world. The homicide rate is from four to 12 times higher that the rate in most industrialized countries, including Canada, England, Japan, Norway and Sweden. It is at least twice as high as its closest competitor, Finland. In the United States, the rape rate is 12 times that of England and Wales and three times that of Canada. The robbery rate is nine times that of England and Wales, and twice that of Canada. And the aggravated assault rate is twice that of England and Wales, and 18 times as high as Canada's.

The Federal Bureau of Investigation's *Uniform Crime Reports,* issued annually, is based on police statistics made available to the agency by the voluntary cooperation of law enforcement agencies throughout the country. The FBI's information, therefore, is based on the number of crimes reported to the police, rather than the number committed. In its annual report for 1968, the FBI reported that nearly 4.5 million serious crimes were recorded for the year; the risk of becoming a victim of serious crime had increased over the preceeding year to the point where there were two victims for every 100 of population; firearms were used to commit 8,900 murders, 65,000 assaults and 99,000 robberies; since 1964 the use of firearms in murders was up by 71 percent, in aggravated assaults by 117 percent, and in armed robberies by 113 percent.

The FBI defines murder, forcible rape, robbery and aggravated assault as crimes of violence. Murder is defined as any willful killing without due process; forcible rape is the carnal knowledge of a female forcibly against her will; robbery is the stealing or taking anything of value from another person by use of force or threat of force; and aggravated assault is the unlawful attack by one person upon another for the purpose of inflicting severe bodily injury, usually accompanied by the use of a weapon or other means likely to produce death or great bodily harm.

It is reported that in 1968 there were more than 13,600 murders or 6.8 for every 100,000 Americans. Forcible rapes totalled more than 31,000 or 15.5 for every 100,000 people. There were more than 261,700 robberies, or 131 for every 100,000. And 282,400 aggravated assaults, or more than 141 for every 100,000 people, were reported.

The incidence of these crimes varied depending upon whether one lived in a large city, a suburban or a rural area; and one was apparently somewhat safer if he lived in the suburbs or a rural area than if he lived in a city. On the other hand, the high incidence of violent crime varied only slightly by region. Southerners are reported to be more prone to murder and aggravated assault, Westerners slightly more likely to commit forcible rape, and residents of the Northeast apt to commit more robberies. Inasmuch as each category represents the incidence of crime reported to the police rather than the actual incidence of the crime committed, it is possible that these variations are less than they appear.

The FBI reports present an elaborate analysis of violent crimes, based on such variables as size of city, region of the country, age, race, type of weapon used and time of year. However, it is sufficient to note that according to their figures a violent crime is committed in the United States every 54 seconds, a murder every 39 minutes, a forcible rape every 17 minutes, and a robbery and aggravated assault every two minutes.

Moreover, it is widely believed that the FBI data represent only a fraction of the actual number of crimes committed in the United States. That is, although police data indicate that crime is widespread, these data do not begin to tell the complete story. In an effort to estimate more accurately the incidence of criminal behavior in the United States, the President's Commission on Law Enforcement and Administration of Justice, appointed in 1965, initiated a national survey of crime victimization. The National Opinion Research Center of the University of Chicago surveyed 10,000 households, asking whether members of the household had been the victim of a crime within the past year. These data were then compared with those reported by the FBI. The results indicate that the actual amount of all crime in the United States is several times that reported by the FBI.

According to the NORC survey, with the exception of murder, the rate of every category of violent crime is much greater than that reported by the police. For example, according to this survey forcible rapes occurred at a rate three and a half times the reported rate, robberies were 50 percent greater, and aggravated assaults were more than double. Even these high rates, the Commission believes, probably understate the actual amounts of crime.

More detailed surveys were conducted in Boston, Chicago and Washington. They tended to support the Commission's contention that the national survey, while giving a more accurate picture of the incidence of criminal behavior than *Uniform Crime Reports,* probably does not give a completely accurate index of the number of crimes committed. The Commission reports that these local surveys, because they were based on interviews with the victims of crime, show even more clearly the discrepancy between the rate of committed crime and that reported by police sources. In Washington the survey results show that the number of offenses ranged from three to ten times more than were reported by the police. The Boston and Chicago surveys indicated that about three times as many crimes were committed as reported by the police.

Although it is not possible to know the real extent of crimes of violence in the United States, violent crime is clearly extensive. It is not surprising that a study conducted by the Commission in two large cities found that nearly half of the respondents (43 percent) stay off the streets at night because of fear of crime, and that more than one-third (35 percent) say they no longer speak to strangers because of the same fear. Nor is it surprising that, as the National Commission on the Causes and Prevention of Violence estimates, there are approximately 90 million firearms in civilian hands in the United States: 30 million rifles, 31 million shotguns, and 24 million handguns. These firearms are kept in some 30 million households.

In many (if not most) big cities, drivers of public busses are not permitted to carry change for passengers for fear of robberies, but in New York City since this practice went into effect there has been an increase in armed robbery of taxi drivers. During the first six months of 1970, six drivers were killed by robbers, and a total of 1,566 robberies were reported. These figures are in contrast to three killings and a total of 1,471 robberies for all of 1969.

Los Angeles and Washington provide examples of what most large American cities have become. In April 1970 the citizens of Los Angeles had hardly recovered from the shock of two mass murders the preceeding year, which accounted for a total of eight lives, when they were shaken by the arrest of five men charged with planning to assassinate a judge who had ordered the city to integrate its public schools. Police found a cache of 250 weapons, including machine guns and grenade launchers, and about 10,000 rounds of ammunition which these right-wingers had stored.

On the same day as the arrest, a Superior Court judge told a court that he was temporarily deranged when he stabbed his wife with a knife. On Thursday of that week a bank robber killed a security guard and an off-duty policeman and was finally killed himself in a shoot-out with other policemen. The following Sunday two white youths who had hiked into the hills with guns for target practice were murdered, apparently by black teenagers who also had guns.

Within a week the following occurrences contributed to the state of panic in Los Angeles. The police killed three citizens: one for holding up a supermarket, another who became abusive and pointed a gun at a policeman, and a professional knife thrower, who held six persons hostage in a bar before being subdued. A 16-year-old boy was accused of murdering his 66-year-old employer, an 81-year-old grandmother was charged with shooting her daughter during a drunken argument, and a 32-year-old man was sentenced to die for beating to death the five year-old son of his common-law wife. Finally, the owner of a store opened fire with a shotgun on six teenagers who had broken into his store earlier and were sitting in a car. One was blinded; another's lung was punctured; two more suffered other wounds. Several days later the owner of the store killed himself with the same shotgun.

The President has called Washington the crime capital of the world. While violent crime in this city appeared to be on the decrease in 1970, the rate had soared between 1966 and 1969. The number of annual homicides, for example, increased from 144 to 289; forcible rapes increased from 134 to 336; robberies from 3,703 to 12,423; aggravated assaults from 3,177 to 3,621; and the number of burglaries increased from 10,267 to 22,992. On Christmas eve of 1969 there were 80 robberies, the highest daily total in the city's history. In fact, the rate of violent crime in Washington has so frightened residents that they are reluctant to leave their homes after nightfall. Several churches have experienced robberies during religious services, and some have hired security guards to protect their collection plates. Many stores and apartment houses have been abandoned for fear of violent crime.

Ironically, when the National Commission on the Causes and Prevention of Violence established offices in Washington in August 1968, several of its staff members became victims of violence in the first six months. One evening a lawyer was mugged and badly beaten downtown. Another was attacked in the lobby of an apartment house. The apartment of still another was robbed, and one young woman was raped and badly beaten in her apartment. Still another was the victim of attempted rape and a successful robbery.

In its final report the Commission predicts a grim future for urban Americans if effective public action is not taken to prevent the drastic increase in violent crime. Some of these predictions are that central cities will be completely abandoned at night except for police patrols; that "high rise apartment buildings and residential compounds protected by private guards will be fortified cells for upper-middle and high-income populations"; that ownership of guns in the suburbs will be virtually universal; that high speed expressways will be "sanitized corridors connecting safe areas, and private automobiles, taxicabs, and commercial vehicles will be routinely equipped with unbreakable glass, light armor, and other security features." In addition, the Commission predicts that "Armed guards will 'ride shotgun' on all forms of public transportation"; that "Armed guards will protect all public facilities such as schools, libraries, and playgrounds"; that slum neighborhoods will be out of the control of the police at night; and that there will be increasing hostility and division between the slum dwellers and those economically able to live in the prosperous "sanitized" areas.

That Americans commit acts of violence against each other on a wide scale is not surprising. The demands of the economic system have created a nation of citizens at war with each other, in a pattern of inequality as glaring as any in modern times. In recent years those at the bottom of the class structure have become aware of this inequality and the degradation which accompanies it, and have begun to strike against the system in any way possible. But since it is frequently impossible to attack the source of the frustration, they indiscriminately brutalize those who are themselves oppressed by the same forces.

Furthermore, the haves in this country have created a legal system which serves their interests and operates against the welfare of the people as a whole. The law is in fact the medium through which inequality is maintained. Naturally the oppressed increasingly defy laws devised to preserve their lowly status. In such circumstances lawlessness has to be rampant, for the law ceases to be based on values representing a consensus of the community.

War

If a people are willing to slaughter their fellow citizens, including members of their own families, it follows that they must be even more willing to kill others. As a cursory look at our past reveals, America, as much as any other nation and considerably more than most, has been a nation at war throughout its history. The earliest settlers immediately engaged in warfare with the Indians they found in North America. Before the Revolution, the colonies came into being and prospered in a state of constant warfare. The Revolutionary War (1775–1783) lasted more than seven years and incurred some 4,435 American battle deaths and another 6,188 wounded, a total of more than 10,000 casualties. Considering the length of the war, the number of casualties was relatively minor, especially when compared with those of wars which were to follow.

The War of 1812 (1812–1815) was the second major war for the United States. Nearly 300,000 U.S. troops were engaged in this effort, with a total of more than 6,700 casualties, including more than 2,200 deaths. The Mexican War (1846–1848) resulted from the annexation of Texas by the United States, and by attempts on its part to purchase New Mexico and California. After its victory, which cost it some 17,000 casualties, the United States annexed more than one million square miles of territory claimed by Mexico, including what is now Arizona, California, New Mexico, Nevada, Utah, and much of Colorado. The Civil War (1861–1865) was one of the bloodiest in American history in terms of total deaths. This war involved more than two million men and caused some 600,000 casualties, half of which were deaths. The Spanish American War (1898) was fought for the ostensible purpose of liberating Cuba from Spain, but its result was that the United States acquired Guam, Puerto Rico and the Philippines and made Cuba a U.S. protectorate. This was a minor war as far as casualties were concerned, with some 2,500 Americans killed and another 1600 wounded.

World War I (1914–1918) was ostensibly fought to defend small nations, and to make the world "safe for democracy." In any case, the Congress of the United States declared war on Germany on April 6, 1917, and nearly five million servicemen were ultimately engaged in battle. The casualty list was high: more than 53,400 Americans killed and more than 200,000 wounded.

World War II (1939–1945) was the last officially declared war in which the United States engaged—that is, it was the last war declared by Congress, the body authorized by the Constitution to commit American forces to warfare. This war, which the United States entered in December 1941, involved more men than any previous war. Altogether some 16 million American troops were mobilized, and by the end of the war the United States had suffered more than a million casualties, including more than 400,000 killed. On a world-wide scale this war lasted for more than six years and was responsible for 30 million deaths among people in and out of uniform; many millions more were injured. Two of the most violent episodes of the war resulted from actions by the United States. On August 6, 1945, America exploded the first atomic bomb over Hiroshima, killing 78,000 people and injuring many times that number. Three days later, on August 9, the Japanese city of Nagasaki was virtually destroyed and 120,000 people were killed by the second atomic bomb. With the explosion of these two bombs the United States killed nearly 200,000 people and injured many times that number.

The Korean War (1950–1953) signalled the first widespread participation by Americans in an undeclared war fought for ideological reasons. The United States had been a major force in establishing the United Nations as an organization for maintaining peace in the world, but later took it upon itself to protect the world from the spread of Communism. Communism was seen as an evil system from which the countries of the world needed protection, and it was assumed that its inevitable spread could be contained by military power. Hence, the United States committed troops to fight in Korea to stop the spread of Communism in Asia. This turned out to be a major war, during which nearly six million troops were mobilized. There were more than

157,000 American casualties, including nearly 55,000 deaths.

The Vietnam War, one of the most bloody in history, was the second major war in which American troops participated without the authorization of Congress. Its purpose, like that of the Korean War, was the containment of Communism, again in Asia. Because of the significance of this war in American history and its widespread domestic consequences, it will be discussed in detail in Chapter III.

These major wars in which America has been involved do not complete the list of actions taken by the government of the United States in an effort to settle political disputes through the use of force. On numerous occasions the U.S. has committed military personnel to combat without a declaration of war by Congress.

In an action which was to become typical, U.S. marines were landed in Hawaii in 1893. They aided in overthrowing the government and establishing Hawaii as a United States protectorate, and in 1898 Hawaii was annexed. In 1900 American troops joined an international expedition in China, the ostensible purpose of which was the protection of foreigners whose legations had been seized by a group of Chinese revolutionaries. In 1903 warships of the United States intervened in Panama when Colombia rejected a proposal for relinquishing sovereignty over the Panama Canal and a minor revolution ensued. The announced purpose was the protection of American interests in the area. The following year (1904), when the government of the Dominican Republic failed to meet debts owed to the United States and other foreign creditors, troops from the United States invaded and effectively controlled the affairs of the country until 1907. Marines were landed in Nicaragua in 1912 when it was felt that there was a possibility of foreign control over the Nicaraguan canal route. They remained until 1933.

An incident involving American sailors in Mexico in 1914 led to the landing of United States troops in that country. In 1916 American Marines imposed a military occupation of Haiti, where they remained until 1934. Mexico was again the target of invasion by American forces in 1916, when raids by Pancho Villa, the guerrilla leader, resulted in the death of Americans on both sides of the border. In the same year the Dominican Republic was again invaded, and this time naval forces remained until 1924.

The American intervention in Korea in 1950 was the first such invasion on so wide a scale. Twenty years after that intervention, 50,000 American troops were still in Korea. In 1958, American Marines were landed in Lebanon for the purpose of forestalling a revolution in that country. In 1965 American troops were again landed in the Dominican Republic, this time to contain what was feared to be a Communist coup.

According to the *Congressional Record,* the armed forces of the United States have been deployed abroad for military action, without the approval of Congress, 163 times between 1798 and 1945. This averages out as more than one act of military intervention per year during this period. The exact number of casualties resulting from these American forays is not known, but millions of persons, civilian and military, have been victims. And, since each case involved the deployment of troops to foreign soil, it is persons other than Americans who have suffered most from American military power. These actions are not likely to end in the near future, either. At the present time the United States maintains a force of more than one million servicemen stationed at some 2,270 military installations in some 30 foreign countries, with an additional one-half million civilian employees and military dependents at these installations.

The total list of casualties resulting from the wars of America includes nearly four million Americans, with more than 600,000 killed, without including perhaps hundreds of thousands of American Indians. Considerably more millions of citizens of other countries, many times the number of American casualties, have also been casualties of these wars.

America's many wars and other military activities have all intended either economic expansion or the maintenance of economic interests at home and abroad. In the past half-century, the United States, with the assistance of its military forces, has created a system in which a tiny fraction of the world's people control more than half its resources. Any attempt to upset this hegemony is inevitably resisted with the full force of history's most destructive arsenal of weapons. Indigenous movements in Third World countries which seek a more equal distribution of the world's resources obviously pose serious threats to America's economic domination of the world, and America must suppress them at all costs.

Moreover, through the years the controllers of America's wealth have succeeded in forcing those who profit least from the maintenance of United States economic interests in the world to slaughter others in its behalf. It has always been the poor and the oppressed who have been killed in disproportionately large numbers in the wars of America. They have been so brutalized and manipulated by the society that they have been willing to fight wars against their own best interests.

Labor Violence

Perhaps as much as any other area in American life, relations between labor and management have been characterized in this country by widespread acts of violence. The history of the labor movement in the United States is the most violent of any industrialized nation in the world, and the violence has not been peculiar to any type of industry, geographic region or specific group.

Although labor violence has been sharply reduced in recent years, at least 700 persons have been killed in American labor disputes, and this is probably a gross underestimation. In addition to these deaths, perhaps hundreds of thousands have been injured. Most of the casualties have been workers striking for the right to organize, although many others have been victims of labor violence. These include one governor (Frank Steunberg of Idaho, killed on December 30, 1905), many union leaders, strikebreakers, soldiers, sheriffs, policemen, women and children. In addition to struggles over the right to organize, labor violence has resulted from attempts by workers to prevent strikebreakers from reopening plants, and by attempts on the part of management representatives and state and federal officials to prevent such interference. In general, a narrow interpretation of property rights is responsible for much of the violence in the labor movement. The major issue seems to have been whether the workers had the right to a voice in determining the conditions under which they were to work or whether the owners of companies had the unqualified right to run their businesses in their own way, without consultation with workers or their chosen representatives.

The first union in America, made up of Philadelphia

shoemakers, was established in 1792, but it was not until 1834 that the first national trade union was organized. Between 1860 and 1869 several more national trade unions were established. By 1880 there were more than 2,400 local unions active in the United States, and some 39 national unions. Organized labor thus had its greatest thrust in the late nineteenth century, and it was during this period that violence became an integral part of the relationship between management and workers.

The 1870's witnessed the beginning of widespread violence in the labor movement, although scattered violence had existed prior to that time. Indeed, this decade was one of the most bloody in American labor history, ending with hundreds dead and thousands wounded. In 1877, by far the most violent year of the decade, railroad strikes began in West Virginia and swept through every major rail center in the United States, affecting virtually all of the railroad mileage in the country. As was generally the case, these strikes resulted from the failure of management to consult workers on matters which directly affected them. In this instance, wages were arbitrarily fixed and lowered by the management of railroads. Railroad strikes and riots ultimately led to many casualties, including more than 30 killed and hundreds wounded in Reading, Pennsylvania, and in Chicago.

The 1880's were less violent than the preceding decade, but again railroad strikes accounted for much of the violence. During this period there were thousands of strikes involving more than two million workers, a number of whom were either killed or injured, but it was in the 1890's that widespread violence again erupted. The right of workers to organize themselves into unions figured in nearly all the strikes of the period. Major strikes involved steelworkers in Pennsylvania, nonferrous metal workers in the West, and railroad workers throughout the country. Hundreds of people were killed in this bloody decade. The Pullman strike of 1894 alone was responsible for 34 killed and hundreds wounded, and in the coal miners' strike in Virden, Illinois, 14 men were killed and hundreds more were wounded.

The twentieth century began with more labor violence. The coal fields of Pennsylvania were the scene of many strikes, several of which erupted into violence. In one county 14 persons were killed and hundreds injured in 1902. In Colorado, striking mine workers throughout the state fought battles with the militia resulting in many deaths and injuries. Transit strikes in New York state, Connecticut, Ohio and Pennsylvania all ultimately led to violence, and in Chicago and New York violent strikes erupted in the clothing industry in 1909 and 1910. In the same years, bloody strikes in the steel industry in Pennsylvania led to a long list of casualties.

During the second decade of the century perhaps more casualties resulted from violence in labor relations than at any other period in this long struggle. Nearly 100 people were killed in the copper strike in Calumet, Michigan, in 1913. In West Virginia at least two dozen strikers and guards were killed in 1912. But it was in the coal industry in Colorado that labor violence resulted in the largest number of casualties.

In 1913 workers in the coal mines of Colorado were the subjects of an organization drive by the United Mine Workers of America, an international union with approximately 400,000 workers in the United States and Canada, which had pledged to extend collective bargaining and industrial democracy to the coal mines. The coal companies, led by the Colorado Fuel and Iron Company, which was controlled by the Rockefeller family through the ownership of 40 percent of its stocks and bonds, refused to meet with representatives of the union. The major issue in the drive for unionization was a demand by the workers for a voice in determining the conditions under which they worked and lived, for the mining companies owned the towns where the workers lived and deprived them of many of the liberties promised by the Constitution. For example, the miners were forced to depend on the company not only for work, but also for shelter, for the purchase of food, clothing and other essentials, for the amount and type of education of their children, and for the right to religious worship. In addition, the mining companies resisted unionization by arbitrarily discharging workers, blacklisting them, and forcing compliance through the use of armed guards, spies and the law enforcement machinery of the state of Colorado.

Prior to the strike, on August 16, one of the company's detectives shot and killed a union organizer in the streets of Trinidad, Colorado. The following month, a convention of miners met in Trinidad and called a strike for September 23. Somewhere between 8,000 and 10,000 miners packed their belongings and took their families to tent colonies which had been established by the union. Conditions in the camps were so miserable that the workers and their families were willing to face a winter in tents in the mouths of canyons.

The day after the strike was called, a marshal was shot and killed, and on October 9 a miner was killed. A party of guards had driven to a tent colony in an armored car, the "Death Special," on which was mounted a machine gun, and they killed the striker and wounded a boy. A few days later guards fired on strikers in the streets, killing three union men. Throughout the following months strikers fought a form of guerrilla warfare with the guards and militiamen. The Colorado National Guard had been sent in toward the end of October, in the service of the Rockefellers who owned the mines, and on April 20, 1914, the Guard destroyed the Ludlow Tent Colony, one of the largest, with rifle and machine-gun fire. Five men and a boy were killed. Eleven women and two children who had taken refuge in a hole under one of the tents burned to death or suffocated after the tents had been set afire. In addition, the Guard assassinated a union leader.

The workers, in response to these acts, declared war on the mining companies and the authority of the state of Colorado as represented by the National Guard. On April 22 armed strikers attacked mine after mine, driving off or killing Guards and setting fire to buildings. By April 29, when federal troops arrived and all fighting ceased, the war in the Colorado mines had claimed a total of at least 74 lives, 50 of them in the last 10 days of fighting. Thousands were injured.

Strikes continued after 1914, but with World War I raging in Europe, the level of labor violence in the United States subsided. Steel and coal strikes, however, were frequent, especially after the war, and during one steel strike in 1919 some 20 people were killed. The efforts of the United Mine Workers of America to organize coal workers resulted in many deaths and injuries in 1919 and 1920. In 1921 at least 21 persons were killed in Logan County, West Virginia, and the next year another 21 were killed during a coal strike in Illinois.

Violence also marked railroad disputes in the 1920's. In some 27 states, in 1922 alone, rail strikes led to violence in which at least 100 persons were killed and thousands injured. The level of violence continued throughout the 1920's and 1930's despite the passage of the National Labor Relations Act in 1935. During the 1930's new types of industries were also involved in violence. Textile workers, steel workers, agricultural workers and longshoremen were all involved either in organizing activity or in strikes during this period, and acts of violence led to a long list of deaths.

As unionization of workers became more widespread and acceptable in the 1940's, labor violence subsided. Organizing and strikes continued, but the number of deaths resulting from these activities declined sharply. Between 1940 and 1946, for example, only about 20 people were killed in labor violence. The Taft-Hartley Act was passed in 1947, and between that year and 1962 only 29 persons were killed in labor disputes.

Violence continues in labor disputes, but it usually results in injuries rather than deaths. Historically, state and federal troops have been called in to quell labor violence, and it has usually been as a result of their intervention that the number of casualties has been so high. Workers on strike, their sympathizers and union organizers have been responsible for a smaller, but not insignificant, amount of the violence which has characterized labor-management relations in American history.

People who try to earn a decent living in the United States are often so brutalized that it is difficult for them to maintain their humanity. Consequently, they brutalize others. Most often, ironically, they brutalize those who are not responsible for their dehumanization, for they are powerless to strike at the real source of their frustrations—the corporate power structure. It is easier for them to kill blacks, students—or members of their own families.

Child Abuse

Children have been abused throughout human history and in all cultures. They have been flogged, mutilated, killed at birth, abandoned and forced into slavery. While most of these extreme practices have been abandoned in most cultures, many other practices, often equally brutal, have replaced them. At the present time violence as brutal as any the human mind is capable of devising is practiced in the United States against countless numbers of children annually.

The number of children in the United States who are the victims of serious physical abuse by parents or adult guardians, frequently resulting in either death or permanent injury, is estimated variously from 10,000 to upwards of 2,000,000 annually. A recently organized study of child abuse at Brandeis University estimated that between 2.3 and 3.7 percent of 110 million adults knew personally of families involved in incidents of child abuse between October 1964 and October 1965. If each of these families knew of a separate incident, this would mean that in that year somewhere between two and four million cases of child abuse occurred in the United States. At the other extreme, the chairman of New York City's Task Force on Child Abuse estimates that the number of children who are brutally mistreated each year totals about 10,000. The New York State Department of Social Services reports that approximately 1,000 cases of child abuse were recorded in 1968 in that state. But in the same year, according to *The New York Times,* the Brooklyn Society for the Prevention of Cruelty to Children reports receiving more than 1,200 complaints in that borough alone.

The Children's Division of the American Humane Association, in a survey of newspapers, found that nearly 700 child abuse cases were reported in 1962. The Brandeis study undertook a press survey for the last six months of 1965, during which they located more than 400 cases. Of that number, 130 incidents involving 164 children were fatal. Finally, in Chicago, the Cook County Family Court reported receiving about 100 cases of child abuse per month in 1962. While the precise extent of child abuse is thus not known, it is clear that it is a widespread phenomenon in the United States. It is likely that reported incidents represent only a small fraction of those which occur, and that the true incidence is more likely to be closer to the estimates of sample surveys.

Adults who abuse children use a variety of instruments and techniques. Children are battered by bare fists, hair brushes, wire coat-hangers, firearms, belts, hot water, chair legs, baseball bats, broom handles, bottles, knives, lighted cigarettes, fan belts, television aerials, ropes, rubber hoses and electric cords. The list is endless and probably includes virtually anything which comes to hand. Often several torture techniques are used against the same child. For example, in one family a young boy was systematically starved, while the other children were permitted to eat. He was burned with lighted cigarettes, beaten with steel wire, and refused all treats and recreation. The mother finally attempted to hang him, and when he was taken to a hospital for treatment he was more dead than alive.

A two-year-old boy died ten minutes after his father took him to a hospital, bleeding from wounds inflicted on his head and body. A 22-month-old youngster was found to be suffering from severe malnutrition, dehydration and congested lungs. When he arrived at the hospital maggots were in his eyes, nose and mouth. The mother of a 29-month-old boy claimed he was a behavior problem and had beaten him with a stick and screwdriver handle, dropped him on the floor, beaten his head against a wall, thrown him against it and choked him to force his mouth open for feeding. When finally the boy was found dead in bed and taken to a hospital, he had burn marks on his face, injuries on his hand and scars from old lacerations covering his body.

As a final instance, in one city a mother became indignant because her 30-month-old daughter did not respond readily to toilet training. In a fit of anger over the child's inability to control a bowel movement, the mother gave her an enema with scalding water. It was necessary for doctors to perform a colostomy to save the child's life.

In a detailed study of 36 children from one month to five years old who died of injuries inflicted by their parents, a Philadelphia forensic pathologist tabulated the ways in which the injuries were inflicted. Some of these follow: "Beat with hair brush," "Struck with vacuum cleaner pipe and fists," "Banged head against wall," "Placed on gas burner," "Immersed in sink of hot water," "Slapped and knocked from table to floor," "Yanked chair from beneath him," "Placed on hot radiator to dry pants," "Beat with wire coat-hanger." In most cases these parents killed their children by striking them with their bare hands.

It is frequently assumed that the parents and guardians who inflict such injuries on defenseless children must be mentally ill. Among those cases which come to the attention of medical doctors, the abusers often suffer from such conditions as retardation, alcoholism and other problems. However, child abuse is so widespread and the data are so inadequate that it is impossible to categorize such parents. Children have been abused because of their illegitimacy, because of hardships caused by the arrival of an unwanted child and because of the failure of a child to live up to the expectations of his parents. A list of some of the reasons parents give for inflicting fatal injuries on their children is filled with trivialities: "Cried too much," "Wet pants," "Would not finish feeding," "Baby was fussy," "Urinated on floor," "Feces smearing," "Drinking sibling's bottle," "Strewing contents of cabinet."

A vast majority of cases of child abuse which reach the courts occur among the poor. This may be due in part to their being forced to use public hospitals and clinics rather than private medical facilities. There is some evidence that child abuse occurs in families of all economic levels, as well as all religious and ethnic groups. Because child abuse is more prevalent among very young children, however, it follows that their abusers are likely to be young parents. In most cases the parents are under 30 years of age. Race does not appear to be a distinguishing characteristic of child abusers, and regionally the incidence of abuse seems fairly representative of the population distribution of the country.

In recent years there have been attempts to curb the abuse of children. Each state now makes it mandatory for physicians to report the case to the appropriate legal authorities when they suspect that children brought in for treatment have been abused. This device is likely to lead to greater prosecution of child abusers and thereby preclude the abuse of other children in the family, but it hardly touches the problem at its source. Violence against defenseless children by parents and guardians is part of the violence in the larger society, and life in most of America is itself a massive act of brutality against people. Social conditions in this country are such that people cannot help but lose their ability to love; child abuse is an extreme expression of this inability.

In addition to widespread violence by parents and guardians against defenseless children, hundreds of thousands of children are physically abused by sadistic officials in so-called correctional institutions throughout the country. And there exist in the United States in 1971 some 800,000 child farm laborers, more than one-third of them the children of migrant farm workers. These children, who are often no more than five or six years old, are a virtual slave labor force. They work as much as 12 hours a day, often in heat exceeding 100 degrees, and are paid absurdly low wages for back-breaking labor. Their plight is hardly different from that of their predecessors in the sweatshops of America prior to the enactment of child labor laws in the 1930's. If the treatment of children is any measure by which a society's humanness can be judged, the United States must be regarded as one of the most barbaric in the industrialized world.

I I I

►►►►►►

Violence in International Relations: Vietnam, An American Atrocity

A people capable of brutalizing their own children are certainly willing to commit extreme acts of cruelty toward others, as the savage behavior of American servicemen in Vietnam shows. Desmond Smith, an American reporter who accompanied American troops on a helicopter inspection tour in South Vietnam, saw an American serviceman at one outpost spraying a human ear with insect repellent. He was ordered by the lieutenant in charge not to film what he had seen. Later he saw the young victim: "His head slumped against the bank, a look of agony frozen beneath the shock of black hair. Both ears had been severed at the root so all that remained were two bloody circles about the size of 50¢ pieces. . . . He didn't look to be more than

15. . . . I remembered that this was the first time I had seen the enemy, and it was just a kid."

Another American observer in Vietnam, William Pepper, described a napalm victim, an eight-year-old boy who survived and was flown to England for treatment. "He came off the plane with a muslin bag over what had been his face. . . . His chin had been 'melted' into his throat, so that he could not close his mouth. He had no eyelids." Both of his parents had been burned alive and after the injury he had had no treatment for four months. The American pilot responsible for this act no doubt never saw his young victim, but the soldier who cut off the ears of the young boy did so with his own hands.

These atrocities need to be put in perspective. The Cold War policy of anti-Communism and containment of wars of national liberation since World War II has forced the United States to intervene in revolutionary struggles the world over—in Bolivia, Colombia, the Congo, Cuba, the Dominican Republic, Guatemala, Korea, Indonesia, Laos and Vietnam. In addition, the United States maintains military installations in some 30 countries around the world, and its Central Intelligence Agency operates in many more. The object of these outposts is the maintenance of American dominance and the support of a policy of opposition to change, especially change which might upset this country's economic interests.

The war in Vietnam is only one manifestation, on a terribly bloody scale, of this policy. Since February 1955 when the first Military Assistance Advisory Group arrived in Vietnam, ostensibly to train the South Vietnamese army, American military personnel have been engaged in acts of violence against the Vietnamese people. The violence intensified with the "limited" air action against the territory of

North Vietnam in 1964, the decision of the President to order continuous air strikes against that territory, and the deployment of combat troops on a large scale into South Vietnam in 1965.

The extent of the destruction caused by America's participation in the war in Vietnam is incalculable. By the end of 1969, American casualties included some 45,000 dead and more than 250,000 wounded. Estimates of Vietnamese casualties run much higher, perhaps totalling well over a million dead and many times that number injured in South Vietnam alone. In the last five years of the 1960's, the United States dropped over three million tons of bombs on Vietnam, more than were dropped in both Asia and Europe during all of World War II.

Moreover, America has introduced into the fighting in Vietnam weapons of destruction more deadly than any previously used in warfare. Chemical warfare has been employed in order to force people out of caves into the open where they can be killed by other weapons. Bullets that expand upon entering the human body are used. Huge amounts of napalm and white phosphorous have been dropped. Napalm not only burns and melts human flesh, but also removes oxygen from the air so that those who escape being burned will die of suffocation. White phosphorous continues to burn its victims even from within the body. Fragmentation cannisters that contain thousands of sharp metal pellets are dropped on civilian populations and lodge themselves deeply in human bodies.

It seems reasonable to say that the type of warfare conducted by the United States in Vietnam represents one of the most violent and brutal examples of warfare in human history, and partly explains the widespread opposition throughout the world to America's involvement. The American conduct of the war in Vietnam, and its widespread acts of gratuitous violence, have been so well documented that large numbers of citizens are convinced it represents a policy of genocide against the people of Vietnam.

While the people of South Vietnam have suffered greater casualties than their counterparts north of the seventeenth parallel, the suffering inflicted on the North Vietnamese has been enormous. For nearly four years, between 1965 and 1968, United States bombers regularly struck the territory of the Democratic Republic of Vietnam, virtually destroying a portion of the most densely populated part of the country. The rationale for this action at first was to force the North Vietnamese into negotiating a settlement of the war. Through the years a series of rationales, including the curbing of infiltration into the South, was offered. Some of the pilots who bombed the North were captured, and when officials of that country implied that captured pilots would be tried as war criminals, there were demands on the part of United States officials that North Vietnam be "bombed off the map."

In addition to violating almost every principle of morality in its conduct of the war in Vietnam, the United States has violated virtually every international principle of the conduct of warfare developed through the years, especially those limiting the degree of violence directed at defenseless civilians. The United States has violated both the Charter of the United Nations and its Universal Declaration of Human Rights. It has violated the Geneva Agreements, ending the war between the French and the Vietnamese, and its own Southeast Asia Collective Defense Treaty. Finally, it has even violated its own Constitution, and a United States Army field manual on the conduct of land warfare.

Three of the international treaties relating to the conduct of warfare to which the United States is party are the Hague Convention of 1907, the Nuremberg Principles of International Law of 1946, and the Geneva Convention of 1949. The Hague Convention states among other things that it is "especially forbidden" to employ poison or poisoned weapons; to kill treacherously individuals belonging to the hostile nation or army; and to kill or wound an enemy who, having laid down his arms, or having no longer means of defense, has surrendered at discretion. Also forbidden is the attacking or bombardment of towns, villages, dwellings or buildings which are undefended.

The Nuremberg principles of International Law, which the United States assumed the leadership in formulating, stipulates three categories of crimes relating to warfare which are punishable under international law: (1) "Planning, preparation, initiation or waging of a war of aggression or a war in violation of international treaties, agreements or assurances"; (2) "Violations of the laws or customs of war which include, but are not limited to, murder, ill-treatment or deportation of slave-labor or for any other purpose of civilian population of or in occupied territory, murder or ill-treatment of prisoners of war or persons on the seas, killing of hostages, plunder of public or private property, wanton destruction of cities, towns, or villages, or devastation not justified by military necessity"; (3) "Murder, extermination, enslavement, deportation and other inhuman acts done against any civilian population, or persecutions on political, racial or religious grounds, when such acts are done or persecutions are carried on in the execution of or in connection with any crime against peace or any war crime."

Several articles of the Geneva Convention of 1949 are relevant to the violence perpetrated by American military personnel in Vietnam: "The parties to the conflict shall take the necessary measures to ensure that children under fifteen, who are orphaned or are separated from their families as a result of the war, are not left to their own resources, and that their maintenance, the exercise of their religion and their education are facilitated in all circumstances. Their education shall, as far as possible, be entrusted to persons of a similar cultural tradition."

"Prisoners of war must at all times be humanely treated. Any unlawful act or omission by the Detaining Power causing death or seriously endangering the health of a prisoner of war in its custody is prohibited, and will be regarded as a serious breach of the present Convention. In particular, no prisoner of war may be subjected to physical mutilation or to medical or scientific experiments of any kind which are not justified by the medical, dental or hospital treatment of the prisoner concerned and carried out in his interest."

"Grave breaches . . . shall be those involving any of the following acts, if committed against persons or property protected by the present Convention: willful killing, torture or inhuman treatment, including biological experiments, willfully causing great suffering or serious injury to body or health, unlawful deportation or transfer or unlawful confinement of a protected person, compelling a protected person to serve in the forces of a hostile Power, or willfully depriving a protected person of the rights of a fair and regular trial prescribed in the present Convention, taking of hostages and extensive destruction and appropriation of property, not justified by military necessity and carried out unlawfully and wantonly."

"At all times, and particularly after an engagement, Parties to the conflict shall, without delay, take all possible measures to search for and collect the wounded and sick, to protect them against pillage and ill-treatment, to ensure their adequate care, and to search for the dead and prevent their being despoiled."

The Charter of the United Nations declares: "All members shall settle their international disputes by peaceful means in such a manner that international peace and security, and justice are not endangered." It directs further that "All members shall refrain in their international relations from the threat or use of force against the territorial integrity or political independence of any state, or in any other manner inconsistent with the Purposes of the United Nations." Finally, the Universal Declaration of Human Rights affirms that "no one shall be subjected to torture or to cruel, inhuman or degrading treatment or punishment."

The Geneva Agreements of 1954 on the cessation of hostilities in Vietnam declared: "With effect from the date of entry into force of the present Agreement, the introduction into Viet Nam of any troop reinforcements and additional military personnel is prohibited. . . . The introduction into Viet Nam of any reinforcements such as combat aircraft, naval craft, pieces of ordnance, jet engines and jet weapons and armoured vehicles is prohibited. . . . No military base under the control of a foreign State may be established in the re-grouping zone of either party; the two parties shall ensure that the zones assigned to them do not adhere to any military alliance and are not used for the resumption of hostilities or to further an aggressive policy."

While the government of the United States refused to sign the Geneva Agreements, its representative issued a unilateral declaration of its position in which it was announced that the United States would "refrain from the threat or the use of force. . . ."

Shortly after the issuance of the Geneva Agreements, the United States and representatives of the governments of Australia, France, New Zealand, Pakistan, the Philippines, Thailand and the United Kingdom met and established the Southeast Asia Collective Defense Treaty of 1954. In this treaty the parties involved pledged to undertake "as set forth in the Charter of the United Nations, to settle any international disputes in which they might become involved by peaceful means in such a manner that international peace and security and justice are not endangered, and to refrain in their international relations from the threat or use of force in any manner inconsistent with the purposes of the United Nations."

According to its own Constitution, treaties to which the United States is party constitute the "supreme law of the land." Therefore, the provisions of these treaties are expected to be observed with the same diligence as other statutes enacted in pursuance of the Constitution. Finally, the Department of the Army's Field Manual, *The Law of Land Warfare,* contains many of the principles of international law which have been violated by American military personnel in Vietnam. This manual reiterates the Principles of the Hague Convention, the Geneva Convention and the Nuremberg Principles. Its purpose is to provide guidance for the conduct of warfare, and "diminish the evils of war" by protecting military personnel and civilians from unnecessary suffering and the safeguarding of the fundamental rights of persons captured in warfare.

Some of the provisions of international laws are no doubt violated during wars by all parties involved. Furthermore, this body of law is hardly enforcible except by the victors over the vanquished after hostilities have ceased. Nevertheless, violations take on added significance when they occur on the part of a country which has played a major role in developing them, and when it, as the most powerful military nation in the world, engages in countless acts of brutality against the people of a small agricultural nation.

The concern here is not with such violations by the Democratic Republic of Vietnam or the forces of the National Liberation Front (NLF), although they occur. Nor is the concern with violations by the government and armed forces of the Republic of Vietnam. American forces represent the largest single group of foreign forces in Vietnam, and it is American personnel, armaments and money which have been responsible for the extraordinary level of violence in Vietnam. The forces of the NLF and its supporters in South Vietnam have no planes, no helicopters, no gunships and no artillery. Nor do they have access to napalm, white phosphorous and fragmentation bombs. These are all weapons utilized by American forces and their supporters.

From all reports civilian casualties in Vietnam exceed those of the military by a ratio of at least three to one, and this is a consequence of the kind of war waged in Vietnam by the United States. That the vast majority of the casualties have been non-combatants—innocent and defenseless women and children—is in itself an example of moral callousness with few parallels in history.

Destruction of Children

An unknown number of children have been killed, burned or otherwise wounded by American actions in Vietnam. William Pepper has estimated that at least one million children had been killed or wounded in South Vietnam alone by the end of 1966, with at last 250,000 children killed. Some of the children killed, wounded or rendered homeless were no doubt victims of military activity by the Vietnamese, but Pepper maintains that a majority of these cases resulted from American military activities. Napalm, white phosphorous, the indiscriminate bombing of villages and bombing accidents account for most of the child victims. Since over 50 percent of the population of South Vietnam is under 16 years of age, a significant proportion of all civilian casualties are children.

While in Vietnam, Pepper interviewed medical officials at hospitals serving war victims. At a hospital in Da Nang he was told by an American medical student that one-fourth of the 800 patients treated each month were burn cases. Of these between 60 and 70 percent were under 12 years of age. Moreover, although the Da Nang Surgical Hospital is one of the best equipped in South Vietnam, it had at this time only one half-pint jar of antibiotic cream, and this was reserved for burned children who had some chance of recovery. Many who did not fall into that category were simply left to die, and the situation at this hospital was typical.

When a Swiss humanitarian organization, Terre des Hommes, sought American assistance in evacuating burned children to Europe, its request was refused. The reason given by a White House official was that children are unhappy when separated from their parents! He put it this way: "However much better a Swiss home or hospital might be, it cannot compensate for having their own families around them in familiar surroundings in their own country." With this rejection, Terre des Hommes turned to commercial airlines for assistance, but the airlines, under pressure from the United States Government, refused free passage for the burned children. Some, however, were later flown to Europe for medical treatment with funds provided by individuals, and others ultimately were brought to the United States under the auspices of another humanitarian organization, the Committee of Responsibility, which has as its concern the treatment and rehabilitation, in the United States, of war-burned Vietnamese children. Nevertheless, by the end of 1969 fewer than 100 children had been brought to the United States for treatment.

On February 19, 1965, a policy of systematically bombing and strafing areas suspected of being strongholds of troops for the NLF was initiated by the United States. Such massive acts of violence against the South Vietnamese probably have accounted for greater civilian casualties than any other military acts. Because of the difficulty in distinguishing between South Vietnamese people loyal to the government of South Vietnam and those loyal to the NLF, the general American practice has been one of simply bombing a village and describing those killed as "Communists." The NLF military tacticians make a point of having their troops live among the civilian population. Therefore, if they are to be bombed it is necessary to bomb civilians as well. According to a reporter from the *New York Times,* when Secretary of Defense Robert McNamara was asked by reporters about the bombing of civilians in Vietnam, he replied that during a five-day visit he had asked many pilots if they were bombing civilians and they all said they were not. But such bombing for more than five years has led to the death of countless thousands of defenseless children. For example, when a village chief called for an American air strike in Truong Thanh because he suspected that NLF forces were sheltered there, two American F-100 Super Sabres showered the village with napalm and bombs. They killed 16 residents, including six children, and wounded another 124.

Dr. Benjamin Spock feels that the war which America is waging in Vietnam is different from any other war in history in that it appears to be conducted against an entire people, including women, children and old men. As a reporter for the *New York Times* put it: "And so, American pilots fan out over the country each day on hundreds of missions. They bomb huts, afterward described as 'structures,' and they kill Vietnamese, afterward described as 'Communists.' "

The American bombing and strafing in South Vietnam commenced in the densely populated Mekong Delta, where the average density is about 250 people per square mile. It is not difficult to imagine the human slaughter caused by these several-times-a-day raids on villages. According to Malcolm Browne, "Sometimes these raids kill enemy guerrillas. Sometimes they merely kill women and children cringing in improvised shelters. Pilots have no way of telling which." Browne cites several cases of bombing accidents between 1966 and 1967. In the village of Lang Vei, after an accidental raid on March 2, 1967, relief workers found 80 civilians dead and 120 wounded. On one occasion, three pilots attempted to empty their unused rockets and bombs into a river, missed their target and bombed a school house, killing eight children and wounding another 52. On October 30, 1965, according to the *New York Times,* when two American planes bombed the "friendly" village of Beduc, some 48 civilians, including women and children, were killed and another 55 wounded. Ten days later the village of Locthuonghiet was also accidentally bombed, killing one woman and wounding ten others, including children.

But not all deaths of children are caused by napalm, bombing raids and accidental bombings. Some of the deaths result from deliberate, sadistic acts of American servicemen. Since children constitute such a high percentage of the population of Vietnam, it is they who are the primary carriers of the culture. And with the extraordinarily high proportion of children killed and maimed, there are particular grounds for calling the war in Vietnam one of genocide.

The attitude of the White House official toward Terre des Hommes is hardly worse than that of many servicemen in Vietnam. To many Americans serving in Vietnam even the children are the enemy. In one village, according to Donald Duncan, a former sergeant who served with the Special Forces in Vietnam, after several women, children and suspected NLF members had been killed, their village set afire, and one captured prisoner needlessly murdered, a newly arrived American sergeant expressed shock at what he had witnessed. His lieutenant turned to him and said: "So a few women and children get killed and a prisoner died under interrogation—tough shit. Teach 'em a damned good lesson. They're all VC or at least helping them—same difference. You can't convert them, only kill them. Don't lose any sleep over those dead children—they grow up to be commies too." Or consider the attitude of a high-ranking American officer in Hue after the Tet Offensive of 1968, who remarked that it was necessary to destroy a village in order to save it. Such attitudes derive from the rigid anti-Communist ethos that pervades the United States and its foreign policy, and they have no doubt contributed to the extraordinary violence from which the children of Vietnam have suffered.

Devastation of the North

In December 1966 Harrison E. Salisbury of the *New York Times* received a visa from the North Vietnamese Government to visit Hanoi and the surrounding area. When his reports indicated that American bombing had not been limited to military targets as had been claimed, and that heavily populated civilian areas had also been bombed, he was severely criticized by officials in Washington, as though his reports had been acts of treason. Readers of the *Times* refused to acknowledge that the destruction Salisbury described had taken place. They did not want to know the truth about their country's policies and the actions of their sons, husbands, friends and neighbors. They were able to ignore the slaughter and to complain instead about the alleged ill-treatment of American pilots whose planes had been shot down and who had been captured as prisoners of war.

Since that time several other American journalists have corroborated the destruction caused by the bombing of North Vietnam. Salisbury himself documented the destruction caused by the bombing of populated areas in Hanoi and the surrounding area. Pho Nguyen Thiep Street, in downtown Hanoi, had been bombed for two days. In one case a single bomb exploded, killing five persons, injuring 11, and destroying 13 houses. In other locations on the street many other persons were killed or injured in the two days of bombing. Schools and religious shrines were also destroyed.

In the village of Phuc Xa, near Hanoi, a single bomb had exploded the previous August, killing 24 persons, wounding another 23, and destroying 24 houses. In addition, bombs wrecked the Polish Friendship School and damaged embassies in Hanoi's diplomatic quarter. One of the more deadly attacks occurred on Hang Thao Street in April 1965. The bombs fell when shifts were changing in factories there, killing 49, injuring 135, and destroying 240 houses. Other streets were completely destroyed in an industrial suburb of Hanoi. In the city of Namdinh, the mayor reported that residences for 12,464 people were destroyed, but casualties were relatively light—only 89 killed and 405 wounded.

The bombing of North Vietnam was especially hurtful for school children. Progress in education had been rapid since the defeat of the French, but the bombing of schools severely handicapped the educational effort. Many pupils were killed. For example, in October 1966 the Thy Dan School, 65 miles south of Hanoi, was struck by four bombs which killed 30 pupils and a teacher. For the safety of the children it was necessary finally to evacuate all schools in population centers.

The suffering inflicted on children by the bombing raids was made clear when Salisbury visited a surgical clinic in Hanoi where 14 children who were victims of a two-day bombing raid were being treated. A ten-month-old girl had suffered a cerebral hemorrhage from a bomb fragment in the brain; a one-year-old boy had a fragment in his skull; an eight-month-old girl had a fragment in her spine and was paralyzed from the chest down; a 16-year-old girl had a bomb fragment in her liver.

Other Western reporters in North Vietnam attest to the destruction caused by the bombing. Wilfred Burchett, an Australian journalist, reported that several hospitals and sanatoria were destroyed and many patients killed. An attack at the Quynh Lap leper sanatorium and research center on June 12, 1965, resulted in 139 deaths and 80 injuries. Harry Ashmore and William Baggs, two American reporters who visited North Vietnam at the beginning of 1967, reported that schools, residential streets and entire villages had been leveled by American bombing. In Nam Dinh, a textile center and the country's third largest city, ten residential blocks had been systematically destroyed.

The Bertrand Russell Peace Foundation financed a trip to North Vietnam by several persons to investigate the American bombing at the end of 1966. The team consisted of observers from France, Japan, Scotland and the United States. When they arrived Hanoi Government ministries provided documents to substantiate their allegations that the United States was guilty of war crimes in North Vietnam. These documents give some indication of the destruction caused by the daily bombing of the territory of North Vietnam. One American, John Gerassi, reported that between February 7, 1965, and June 30, 1966, some 170 raids had taken place against hospitals, sanatoria and infirmaries. A total of 80 establishments, containing more than 9,000 hospital beds, had been bombed and strafed. One leper sanatorium had been bombed 39 times. By the end of September 1966, it is reported that 294 schools, ranging from nurseries to teachers' colleges, were bombed and strafed, usually when classes were being held. During this period 331 pupils were killed and 172 others wounded. Some 35 teachers were killed and 32 wounded.

The bombing of North Vietnam ended on November 1, 1968. In the nearly four years of constant bombardment American pilots flew nearly 100,000 missions and dropped more than one million tons of bombs. This is roughly twice the tonnage used in the entire Pacific theater during World War II. It is difficult to determine the damage caused by these bombs, but Michael Maclear, a Canadian journalist, writing in the Chicago *Daily News,* estimated that approximately 100,000 civilians had been killed. Countless others were injured, especially as a result of napalm and fragmentation bombs. Moreover, that the casualty list is not higher is due to the ingenuity of the North Vietnamese people—men, women and children—who, over the years of warfare, have developed techniques for the rapid evacuation of the population. It was ultimately necessary for them to evacuate most of the population centers of the country, forcing the people to move to caves in the hills from which they had fought the Chinese through the centuries and, more recently, the French.

During his stay in North Vietnam, Michael Maclear attempted to make an over-all assessment of the damage caused by the bombing. The area hardest hit, he reported, was the southern panhandle of the country, stretching for more than 1,000 miles from Hanoi to the Demilitarized Zone. It is also the most densely populated section of the country, formerly containing one-third of the 17 million people of North Vietnam. In this area the five principal cities, all with populations between 10,000 and 30,000, were either completely leveled or rendered uninhabitable. Another 18 towns with populations between 3,000 and

5,000 were completely destroyed. In other words, the most populous section of the country, with most of North Vietnam's urban centers, was destroyed by the bombing. North Vietnamese guides talked to Maclear about the "lost century," meaning that whatever the French had accomplished in 80 years of occupation, and whatever the Democratic Republic of Vietnam had built in some 15 years of uneasy independence, was no longer recognizable. In four years of bombing, the Government of the United States nearly succeeded in fulfilling the proposal of retired Air Force General Curtis LeMay, that North Vietnam be bombed back "to the stone age," and the suggestion of California governor Ronald Reagan that the entire country be leveled into a parking lot.

Inasmuch as there was no declaration of war by the United States against the Democratic Republic of Vietnam, and no attack on the United States by troops from that country, the systematic devastation of a people and their culture by the world's mightiest military power must stand as one of the most grotesque acts of violence in human history.

Bombing Villages and Torturing Prisoners

Nevertheless, the destruction caused by nearly four years of systematically bombing the territory of North Vietnam hardly compares with what has happened in the South. The United States Air Force has dropped more than three million tons of bombs on the South, and in January 1969 alone, some 130,000 tons of bombs were dropped, equaling twice every week the power of the bomb dropped on Hiroshima. Countless thousands of non-combatants, usually women and children, have been killed in the bombing and strafing of villages. And since 1965, when the American government admitted that gases were being used in South Vietnam, more than 7,000 tons of gas have been used. These gases force the people out into the open so that they can then be killed by other means. In addition, anti-plant chemicals have devastated all life in a significant portion of the country. To accomplish this destruction, the United States has assembled the most extensive force of air weaponry ever known. Frank Harvey's catalogue of the instruments of destruction used by the Air Force includes more than 50 different types of aircraft, ranging anywhere from the giant intercontinental B-52 bombers, originally designed for use against the Soviet Union, to the smallest helicopters. Tan Son Nhut airport in Saigon and the one in Da Nang are said to be two of the busiest airports in the world.

The bombing of villages in South Vietnam usually takes place because of reports that NLF soldiers have been sheltered there. Frequently these reports are without foundation, but the A-IE's, B-57's, F-100's, F-105's and the giant B-52 superbombers deposit their cargoes of bombs on the villages. James Pickerell, a reporter sympathetic to American participation in the war, wrote, "There are no statistics available on how many people—VC or innocent peasants—are hit by these bombing attacks. Calculations by anyone are pure conjecture." Air Force fliers are instructed to bomb populated areas as little as possible, but they frequently do not follow these instructions, and sometimes they are given faulty information. While the crews of some of the smaller aircraft are able to see their targets, thereby possibly concentrating on military areas, the crews of the B-52's cannot see their targets from altitudes of at least 30,000 feet, and frequently bomb non-combatants. Even when a visible target is clearly not military, a pilot may choose to bomb it or may be ordered to do so. For example, an American reporter in Vietnam recalls that he was a passenger on a bombing raid when the Forward Air Controller pilot was instructed by radio from the ground that a large Buddhist shrine in the middle of a rice paddy was believed to be a haven for NLF forces. "We'd like to have you lay [some bombs] in as close as you can. If you hit it, don't worry. If anybody says anything, we saw a bunch of them [the enemy] run in there." The callousness and even diligence with which American pilots deposit their bombs on noncombatants in Vietnam suggests an urge to completely destroy the country, no matter what justification officials in Washington conjure up for the war in Vietnam.

In the first eleven months of American bombing of South Vietnamese territory, the Air Force dropped more than 56,000 tons of bombs on villages, and the South Vietnamese Air Force dropped another 25,000, a total more than the French dropped during their entire Indochinese war. During this period it is estimated that more than 200,000 structures were destroyed by the bombings. It is the opinion of Victor Knoebl, an Austrian journalist who travelled extensively in Vietnam, that "The civilian population suffers more from the bombs than the guerrillas do, for the Viet-Cong is trained and accustomed to living a spartan and dangerous existence. The Viet-Cong can retreat to hideouts in the dense rain forests, but the peasants cannot escape the planes. . . ."

In the autumn of 1966 Bertrand Russell issued a call for an International War Crimes Tribunal to meet in 1967, to decide whether or not war crimes were being perpetrated by Americans in Vietnam. One of the areas which this Tribunal investigated was, "the bombing of hospitals, sanatoria, schools, dikes, and other civilian areas." Evidence of such bombings in North Vietnam had been clearly established, and reports of bombing of civilian areas in the South have appeared with such frequency in American and other Western newspapers as to remove any doubt that by such activity the United States had violated not only the Nuremberg Principles of International Law, relating to "wanton destruction of cities, towns, and villages," but also virtually every other principle of the laws of war. And in addition to the indiscriminate bombing of towns and villages in South Vietnam, the American Navy engaged in the systematic bombardment of coastal villages, often in areas where no fighting was underway.

After travelling in South Vietnam, Mary McCarthy gave a graphic description of the American bombing: "A short trip by helicopter from Saigon in almost any direction permits a ringside view of American bombing. Just beyond the truck gardens of the suburbs, you see what at first glance appears to be a series of bonfires evocative of Indian Summers; thick plumes of smoke are rising from wooded clumps and fields." Farther away from Saigon, the bombing is even more intense. The skies over Vietnam are saturated with planes dropping their cargoes of bombs, and the large number of Vietnamese in the refugee camps in the South is more a response to American bombing than to fear of the guerrillas.

In addition to the bombing of villages from high altitudes, low-flying aircraft regularly strafe villages. The strafing is as indiscriminate as the bombing because it is impossible to distinguish combatants from non-combatants, except in cases where the aircraft has been fired upon. An area may be declared a "free bomb zone," within which all people are declared to be "enemy" military forces. Such areas are systematically bombed and strafed by low-flying aircraft in missions called "skunk hunting" by American forces.

One of the main reasons for the high ratio of civilian casualties on strafing missions is that as soon as helicopters and other low-flying aircraft appear over a village, the peasants tend to flee, and fleeing peasants are assumed to be guerrillas and shot down. In the first years of the war the casualty rate for civilians in such circumstances was very high, but the guerrillas soon counselled peasants working in the fields to stand motionless when American aircraft appeared, thereby saving their lives.

The humane treatment of prisoners of war is one of the basic rules of law in the conduct of warfare. While it is likely that all countries accord prisoners of war less than humane treatment under certain circumstances, news dispatches and books written by newsmen and other observers in South Vietnam attest to the extreme cruelty to which prisoners of war are subjected by American and South Vietnamese forces.

According to Victor Knoebl, "The interrogation of prisoners is usually rough in war, but in Viet-Nam it is often a matter of overwhelming cruelty. One method used to make a prisoner talk is to tie slip-knotted cords around his throat and feet, so that if the man moves, the noose around his throat tightens. Then he is laid in a rice paddy, where the water is no deeper than eight inches. The prisoner can keep from drowning by raising his head; but the noose around his throat draws tighter at every movement of his head. Within fifteen or twenty minutes he has strangled himself. Another method is to hang a captive by the feet over a rain barrel and slowly submerge him in it. He is not kept under long enough to drown at first; the process is repeated until the man talks or dies."

Donald Duncan described a grim murder of a prisoner: "Mon, the tall Vietnamese platoon leader, straddles the dying youth's thighs and drives a large knife into his bloody gut, extending the opening in one upward slash. The prisoner rises off the ground, rigid and arched from the waist, face distorted, eyes bulging, screaming like all the horrors of hell. Mon's face flashes annoyance and he slams a backhanded fist into the unhuman face, knocking the body flat, and continues his butchering. The body gives a few jerks, quivers, is still. Mon shoves his hand into the stinking hole and brings out the gall bladder. Grinning triumphantly, he holds his gory trophy overhead for all to see." Present at this event were an American lieutenant, and two noncommissioned officers, all members of the Special Forces. When one of the enlisted men protested, the lieutenant replied: "Don't interfere. It's their show. . . . Sergeant, there's an old saying, 'If you can't stand the heat, get out of the kitchen.' "

Newsweek reported that "In one place, the GIs came upon three wounded North Vietnamese. One lay huddled under a tree, a smile on his face. 'You won't smile anymore,' snapped one of the soldiers, pumping bullets into his body. The other two met the same fate."

The Chicago *Sun-Times* published two photographs in 1969 showing a prisoner of war being dropped to his death from an American helicopter. The photographs were made by a pilot flying escort for a command and control ship. He wrote on the back of the first photograph: "Uncle Nguyen takes a look at the world from 5,000 feet—upside down. I would imagine he's a little upset about now, but not as upset as he'll be in a few minutes. I was in radio contact with the CC ship and John, the pilot, was keeping me informed. I could hear this guy screaming when John keyed his mike." On the second photograph, showing the man falling to his death, he wrote: "And here he takes a sky dive without the aid of a parachute. My ship followed him down and we found him. The picture isn't too pretty, but the whole episode had good results as the other two 'Charlies' told us everything we wanted to know. I bet they were nervous.

Next day four arms caches were found as a result of this incident."

According to the *New York Times,* "One American helicopter crewman returned to his base in the central highlands . . . without a fierce young prisoner entrusted to him. He told friends that he had become infuriated by the youth and had pushed him out of the helicopter at about 1,000 feet."

Malcolm Browne reported that "Vietnamese troops have taken their share of enemy heads over the years, and many Americans have adjusted to the idea. At one point, many of the American advisors returning from Viet Nam brought photos of themselves holding aloft freshly severed heads given them by Vietnamese colleagues. The Americans in the pictures generally were smiling at their heads, as they would at a good catch of fish."

In the early stages of American participation in the war in Vietnam, the policy was that captured prisoners and suspected guerrillas should be turned over to the South Vietnamese army for interrogation and custody. Because of the brutality of the South Vietnamese troops, the policy was changed in mid-1966, and prisoners were sent to American installations until they could be transferred to new prisoner-of-war compounds. In many cases, however, the treatment prisoners met at the hands of the Americans was no different from what they had received from the South Vietnamese.

Murder and torture have not been practiced by the majority of American military personnel in Vietnam. Indeed, many young servicemen have expressed shock at the killing of prisoners, as they have at the murder of innocent civilians. Many American servicemen have, in fact, become opposed to what they see as a civil war in Vietnam. Such opposition was expressed in an advertisement in the *New York Times* supporting the November 1969 peace activities in the United States. This advertisement, signed by 1,365 American servicemen on active duty, including 190 serving in South Vietnam at the time, read in part: "We are opposed to American involvement in the war in Vietnam. We resent the needless wasting of lives to save face for politicians in Washington."

But for the vast majority of servicemen stationed in Vietnam, as well as their fellow citizens back home, the Vietnamese people are not human beings at all, and their murder and torture are accepted nonchalantly, as comparable acts against blacks and Indians have been accepted over the centuries.

Massacres

In any war, declared or undeclared, civilians are likely to suffer, but the war in Vietnam reveals an extraordinary level of violence against Vietnamese people not involved in combat. There are many reasons for this. In the first place, it is difficult to distinguish between individuals loyal to the NLF and those loyal to the American-supported Government of South Vietnam. Having been taught that they were in Vietnam to kill "commies," Americans frequently pursue their goal with a zeal transcending all rationality. In other words, they have internalized the anti-Communist ethos, which has pervaded the United States since World War II, to the degree that anyone suspected of being a Communist is frequently killed first and later declared to have been a supporter of the NLF.

But probably the most important factor accounting for the numerous American massacres of civilians in Vietnam is that the Vietnamese are "slant-eyed gooks" to many American servicemen and therefore less than human. It is impossible for people who have grown up in a society where nonwhites are depreciated in all walks of life to free themselves completely from the racist values they have learned since early childhood. Even the Vietnamese fighting on the same side is still just another "gook." Many comments about the Vietnamese by American servicemen attest to the depth of their prejudice. For example, an American major in South Vietnam was asked by Jonathan Schell how he felt about serving with soldiers from the South Vietnamese army. "I just can't take it any longer," the major said. "You can't get anything done with these Arvins [soldiers of the South Vietnamese army], and I'm going out of my mind. I've applied for reassignment to work with our own men again." A sergeant who worked with the major said, "I've worked, eaten and slept with these villagers for six months, and I want to tell you I have no sympathy for these people, I really don't." Still another sergeant, when asked whether civilians were not occasionally killed in the bombings, replied, "What does it matter? They are all Vietnamese."

An American serviceman expressed the attitude of many when he said, "A lot of guys feel that they [South Vietnamese civilians] aren't human beings." Donald Duncan has written that when he was training to be a recruiter for the Special Forces, his final instructions from the captain in charge of the program were: "Don't send me any niggers." It is difficult to imagine how people with these views could feel differently about the Vietnamese. This former sergeant, who also spent time in South Vietnam, summed up the attitudes of most Americans toward the Vietnamese: "Contact with the Vietnamese . . . was restricted to the essential minimum. Other than counterparts and officials with whom they reluctantly did business, the only Vietnamese the Americans had contact with were the taxi drivers and the bar-girls."

Several other American reporters and observers report the extent of prejudice held by American servicemen toward the Vietnamese people. According to Raymond Coffee in the Chicago *Daily News,* ". . . despite all the years of official talk about the importance of 'winning the hearts and minds' of the Vietnamese people, the most evident and most profound feeling toward the Vietnamese among GIs is contempt. South Vietnamese may be brave and loyal allies in the political rhetoric of Washington, but they are 'gooks' and 'slopes'—and draft dodgers, deserters, slackers—in the view of many GIs." Sociologist Charles Moskos, Jr., reports that "The low regard in which the Vietnamese—'slopes' or 'gooks'—are held is constantly present in the derogatory comments on the avarice of those who pander to GIs, the treachery of all Vietnamese, and the numbers of Vietnamese young men in the cities who are not in the armed forces." After her trip to Vietnam Mary McCarthy wrote that "To some of the men fighting in Vietnam, naturally, there are no good Vietnamese except dead ones." She believes that much of the contempt Americans feel for the Vietnamese results from their watching soldiers of the South Vietnamese army torture other South Vietnamese suspected of being guerrillas or supporting the NLF.

The contempt most American servicemen hold for the people of Vietnam explains why the Vietnamese are likely to be the objects of violence to which Europeans and other people of European ancestry would, in all likelihood, be spared. The question of whether the Government of the United States would systematically destroy the people and culture of a nation of white persons has been pointedly raised in many Third World nations, and given the history of American racism, both at home and in the conduct of foreign affairs, the question is not inappropriate.

Racism explains at least partly the atrocities Americans

have committed in Vietnam. One such atrocity, as reported by Norman Poirier, occurred in the little hamlet of Xuan Ngoc the evening of September 23, 1966. Nine men of the First Squad of the Second Marine Platoon ventured away from the area they were patrolling into the hamlet of Xuan Ngoc in the early morning hours. They approached a hut in which a 61-year-old man, his 70-year-old wife, his two sisters and two nieces were sleeping. The Americans accused the family of being Communists, but they produced identification papers to prove otherwise. The old man was then pulled from the bed by his hair, kicked in the stomach and led with his family into the fields where all six were terrorized for ten minutes. The old man was repeatedly kicked and struck with rifle barrels. His hut was destroyed.

At the next hut a 38-year-old man was asleep with his wife and five children. Several Marines beat him until he was too weak to stand, while others covered the bunk in which the children slept with pieces of firewood. After terrorizing the parents by pretending to burn their children, the Marines left.

The occupants of the next hut, having heard the screams of the terrorized peasants, had taken shelter in a rear bunker. When the Marines arrived at the bunker they forced out a 16-year-old girl and two older women. The Marines grabbed the 16-year-old girl, ripped her clothes off, forced her legs open, and a medical corpsman inspected her with a flashlight. Fearing that she had venereal disease, they left.

The Marines then raided six more huts, in each case beating and terrorizing the peasants. By the time they reached the tenth hut they were frustrated and angry because they had found neither weapons nor NLF soldiers or supporters. At this hut they found six people asleep, including an 18-year-old woman, her husband, and their three-year-old son. They beat the husband and pulled the three other persons from the hut. When they found a hand grenade in the house, they rounded up the occupants and took the 18-year-old woman to the side of the hut, where five of them raped her. The other members of the family could hear her screams but were powerless to help. When her husband protested, they killed him, his wife, his mother and one child. The Marines then left but returned later and killed another child.

This massacre left five innocent people dead, dozens wounded and a village completely destroyed. When the events which took place in this village ultimately came to the attention of military authorities, they investigated and the Marines were eventually tried and convicted for the murders and the rapes. Two of them were still in prison three years later, six of them were back in civilian life, and the ninth member of the First Squad was still a sergeant in the Marine Corps.

Perhaps the most appalling massacre, in terms of the number of people involved, occurred in the village of Mylai 4, also known as "Pinkville" by American servicemen, in the northern part of the country, on March 16, 1968. Reports of this massacre have been published in books by Richard Hammer and Seymour Hersh, and the resultant charges and trials were widely covered by the news media. The complete facts of the events at Mylai 4 may never be known, but more than 500 civilians—men, women and children—may have been murdered in one of the most brutal acts of violence in the Vietnam War. Some observers estimate that as few as 102 people were killed; most estimates, including those of the few surviving villagers who managed to avoid death because the bodies of their friends, relatives and neighbors fell on them and shielded them from the bullets, put the number of deaths at 567.

The deliberate, methodical murder of these civilians was carried out by the 60 or 70 men in the Third Platoon of C

Company, First Battalion, 20th Infantry Regiment, 11th Brigade, of the Army of the United States. This massacre came to public attention when an ex-soldier sent a letter to the President, the Secretary of Defense, 23 Congressmen, and several other government officials, indicating that "something rather dark and bloody" had occurred at Mylai. While he was not party to the massacre, he wrote that friends who were present had told him that orders had been given to "slaughter all the inhabitants of the village," and that many of the men obeyed the orders. Since that time photographs of hundreds of dead civilians have appeared in American newspapers, and soldiers who were present in the village at the time have recounted the events of the mass slaughter.

One veteran described what happened to a group of the villagers: "They had them in a group standing over a ditch —just like a Nazi-type thing. One officer ordered a kid to machine-gun everybody down, but the kid just couldn't do it. He threw the machine-gun down and the officer picked it up. . . . I don't remember seeing any men in the ditch. Mostly women and kids." After all of the villagers were thought to have been killed, their houses were either burned or blown up.

Another soldier, a sergeant who was ostracized for his refusal to participate and who was ordered not to discuss the events, recalls that most of the victims were women, children and old men. "They [the infantrymen] would get the people together and gather them in groups. Then they would shoot them with rifles and machine guns. Going through the village I saw a lot of bodies in these things that looked like bomb craters. I actually saw them shoot some of them. I saw them shoot a group in a ditch, about 20 of them." When asked if there had been any NLF forces in the village, he replied: "Some of the people weren't old enough to walk yet, so I couldn't see how they could be Vietcong."

An American photographer reports: "I remember this man distinctly holding a small child in one arm and another child in the other, walking toward us. They saw us and were pleading. The little girl was saying, 'No, no' in English. Then all of a sudden a burst of fire, and they were cut down."

An ex-sergeant reported: "I passed a ravine which is just before you hit the village. And there were a lot of males and some females lined up there on the edge of it. Our platoon moved away, back into another part of the village. When I came by that ravine 30 minutes later, most of the people were in the ditch. And they were dead or were dying." The sergeant recalled that most of the killing was done by what he called the younger "dumb kids" in the platoon who "went crazy."

Another veteran of the Mylai 4 massacre admitted his role in these events in a nationwide radio interview. He said he killed 10 or 15 men, women and children, including babies. When they arrived in the village, he reported that 45 or 50 Vietnamese people were huddled together in the center of the village. The lieutenant in charge is reported to have said, "You know what to do with them, don't you?" The soldier reports that he understood they were to be guarded, but that the lieutenant returned and asked, "How come you ain't killed them yet?" When the soldier said he did not know they were to be killed, the lieutenant said, "I want them dead." The order was carried out.

The same veteran reports having participated in pushing 70 to 75 men, women and children into a ravine where they were all shot with automatic rifles. During this massacre the soldiers were told "to switch off to single shot so that we could save ammo. So we switched off to single shot, and shot a few more rounds." When asked what the Vietnamese civilians were saying during the massacre, he replied: "They was begging and saying 'No, no.' And the mothers was hugging their children and begging, but they kept right on firing. Well, we kept right on firing. They was waving their arms and begging."

Throughout the interview the veteran referred to the Vietnamese people as "gooks." At no point did he call them by any other name. He said that at the time of the interview he was the father of two young children, and when asked how he could shoot babies, he replied: "I don't know. It just seemed like the natural thing to do at the time." He attributed his behavior to a desire for revenge for friends who were killed and wounded in Vietnam. Upon learning that he had been involved in the massacre, his mother is reported to have said, "I sent them a good boy and they made him a murderer."

Still another veteran of the massacre reported in an interview that he killed ten people in Mylai 4, including one woman and a two-year-old child. When asked how he felt about what had happened, he replied: "I don't think all that should have happened—all those people." He claims not to have participated in group killings, but reports having seen about 25 persons, including some babies, lying dead in a group. He said in an anguished tone that "I think something is going to happen to me. I dream about it a lot. Sometimes I just want to get away from people." It is ironic that this veteran is a young black college student from Jackson, Mississippi.

From all accounts the American soldiers involved in the Mylai massacre were motivated to commit such acts, at least in part, by deeply rooted prejudices against the Vietnamese people. Had they seen these people as human beings it is doubtful that they could simply have annihilated them. They were "dirty gooks," and some of them were suspected of being "commies"; the combination reduced them to a status less than that of human beings. In response to an editorial on the massacre, a reader telephoned the *Chicago Daily News* to say: "Those people over there are a bunch of Commies anyway and they all deserve what they got—every man, woman and child of them—" in an attitude reminiscent of the attitudes of many Americans about the slaughter of blacks and Indians.

Support for this assertion is provided in the results of a Harris poll conducted for *Time* magazine in December and reported in the January 12, 1970, issue of the magazine. A nationwide cross section of Americans were asked how they felt about the massacre at Mylai 4. Nearly two-thirds (65 percent) simply shrugged off the massacre, saying that "incidents such as this are bound to happen in war." As the *Chicago Daily News* editorialized: "So one stark fact to be regarded in the Pinkville affair is that it is not necessarily the end of a story: it could just as well be the beginning. For the supply of 'Gooks' is practically endless; they comprise most of the people of the world. Many of them are also 'Commies,' or at least live under Communist governments." The guilt for the Mylai 4 massacre must be shared by all those Americans who see black people and other non-whites as "gooks," "niggers," and other less than human creatures.

But these publicized massacres represent only a few of the many which American servicemen have committed against the Vietnamese people. Young Vietnamese girls have been kidnapped, raped and murdered by American patrols. While public officials, including the President, assert that the Mylai murders form an "isolated incident," evidence continues to mount indicating it was bùt one of many similar atrocities which have become an integral part of the conduct of the war. Commenting on the events at Mylai 4, Bertrand Russell had this to say: "The revelations of atrocities by U.S. servicemen in Viet-Nam illustrate not isolated acts inadvertently committed by disciplined troops, but the general pattern of the war, for its character is genocidal." Two American reporters, who six months before the massacre spent several months in the province in which Mylai 4 is located, witnessed the province being destroyed. In August 1967, they report, "the 'pacification' camps became so full that Army units in the field were ordered not to 'generate' any more refugees." Peasants were simply killed in their villages because there was no more room in the pacification camps. "Village after village was destroyed from the air as a matter of *de facto* policy. Airstrikes on civilians became a matter of routine."

A reporter for the *New Yorker* magazine described how a village in the same area had been saturated with psychological warfare leaflets entitled, "The U. S. Marine Ultimatum to Vietnamese People." It read, "The U. S. Marines issue this warning: THE U. S. MARINES WILL NOT HESITATE TO DESTROY, IMMEDIATELY, ANY VILLAGE OR HAMLET HARBORING THE VIETCONG. WE WILL NOT HESITATE TO DESTROY, IMMEDIATELY, ANY VILLAGE OR HAMLET USED AS A VIETCONG STRONGHOLD TO FIRE AT OUR TROOPS OR AIRCRAFT." The leaflets went on to list several villages which had been destroyed.

It is likely that other massacres will be uncovered, and if the Nuremberg Principles of International Law are as applicable to Americans after the war in Vietnam as they were to the Germans after World War II, war crimes trials could continue into the indefinite future. In the meantime, the people of Vietnam and their culture will have been virtually destroyed. In the meantime, also, the young men who have been trained to kill indiscriminately in Asia, and who have been rewarded for this behavior by their government, will have returned to the United States as civilians. Can they somehow be expected to erase this experience from their lives? Or will "niggers" and "spics" become the "gooks" of the United States?

I V

►►►►►►

Violence in Domestic Relations: Persecution of Black and Red People

The black uprisings in American cities in the last half of the 1960's, with their massive destruction of property, terrified many white Americans. Little attention was paid to the hundreds of black people—men, women and children—who were killed by police and National Guardsmen for such minor acts as looting stores or simply being present during what have come to be known as "civil disorders." The black man is seen by many white Americans as the most violent member of the society, yet the number of deaths and injuries resulting from the actions of black people represent a small fraction of all persons killed or injured in the United States. What emerged from the urban uprisings of the 60's was typical of the history of American race relations: the slaughter of nonwhite people by white people. These uprisings differed from earlier race riots in that they were not direct clashes between black and white people, but in terms of the number of black people killed, the results were similar.

One of the most pervasive themes in the history of American race relations is the systematic destruction of black and red people by white people. Blacks and Indians were not, however, the only racial minorities to encounter extensive violence from Americans of European ancestry. There were frequent massacres of Chinese railroad and mining workers in the West during the second half of the nineteenth century. For example, a mob of white persons raided the Chinese community in Los Angeles in 1871, killing 19 persons and leaving 15 of them suspended from scaffolds to serve as a warning to survivors. And in Rock Springs, Wyoming, during a railroad strike in 1885, white workers stormed the Chinese community and murdered 16 persons, leaving all their homes burned to the ground. Predictably, a coroner's jury ruled that the victims had been killed by unknown parties.

The Chinese were brought to the United States to be used as slave laborers in the mining and railroad industries on the West Coast. When white workers felt that the Chinese were a threat to their precarious economic position, they resorted to violence. And although there were laws to protect Chinese immigrants, it was in the economic interest of the mine and railroad owners to keep the Chinese divided from white workers by ignoring or suspending these laws. This technique effectively served to keep all workers oppressed and controlled.

Violence against the Chinese subsided with the enactment of legislation excluding them from the country. When Japanese immigration increased toward the turn of the twentieth century, they replaced the Chinese, who withdrew to the relative safety of urban Chinatowns, as objects of American brutality. Mexican immigrants in the West and Southwest faced the same terror and violence which has historically characterized the meeting of Americans of European ancestry and people of other races.

The present chapter, however, is concerned only with acts of violence against black and red people throughout American history. These two groups of people have been subjected to greater persecution than any others in the society, and that they have managed to survive such barbaric treatment can only be attributed to their extraordinary fortitude.

Black People

The institution of slavery in North America was a massive act of violence against black people. Even before the Africans were shipped to what is now the United States, the capture of the slaves in Africa and the Middle Passage were both brutal processes. Estimates vary of the number of blacks who were killed or tortured to death before they reached North America, but it could well have been many millions. My concern here, however, is with what these people were subjected to after their arrival in America.

Slavery

While earlier scholars often attempted to minimize the brutality of slavery, revisionist historians have described the institution as one of the most brutal forms of social relations ever to exist. In part, the nature of North American slavery derived from the definition of the black man as less than human. He was the private property of the slaveholder, and owners of slaves had virtually unlimited power over their property. Of course, since few slaves accepted the slaveholders' definition of their status, they were a "troublesome property." And as a means of maintaining absolute control over their slaves, the slaveholders did not hesitate to resort to violence, most commonly in the form of beatings.

Although slaveholders frequently stopped short of murder, since slaves were valuable property, many a slave met his death at the hands of his owner. The violence of the institution of slavery was vividly described by ex-slaves who were interviewed about their experiences in 1937 by B. A. Botkin. A 90-year-old man described in detail the chaining of a group of slaves to horses in Georgia and their forced march to Texas. They were forced to make the long journey, often through snow, without shoes.

> Massa have a great, long whip platted out of rawhide, and when one of the niggers fall behind or give out, he hit him with that whip. It take the hide every time he hit a nigger. Mother, she give out on the way, 'bout the line of Texas. Her feet got raw and bleeding, and her legs swoll plumb out of shape. Then massa, he just take out he gun and shot her, and whilst she lay dying he kicks her two-three times and say, "Damn nigger what can't stand nothing." Boss, you know that man, he wouldn't bury mother, just leave her laying where he shot her. You know, there wasn't no law 'gainst killing nigger slaves.

Few adult slaves escaped some form of sadism at the hands of slaveholders. A female slaveholder was widely known to punish her slaves by beating them on the face. Another burned her slave girl on the neck with hot tongs. A drunken slaveholder dismembered his slave and threw him piece by piece into a fire. Another planter dragged his slave from bed and inflicted a thousand lashes on him.

According to Kenneth Stampp, a majority of the slaveholders relied on the certainty of physical punishment as the most effective means of controlling slaves. The whip, made of rawhide or cowskin, was an instrument of extreme brutality, and an elaborate system developed in which the number of lashes meted out depended upon the alleged offense charged against the slave. Minor offenses, such as being late for work in the fields, subjected slaves to a few lashes; more serious offenses, such as drunkenness, usually resulted in many more lashes. Women frequently used the whip on domestic servants.

In addition to the slaveholders, white overseers frequently flogged slaves. Some of them, upon assuming control, whipped every slave on the plantation as a means of establishing their authority. In many ways, slaves on plantations with overseers experienced greater brutality than their counterparts on smaller plantations which did not employ these landless poor white tyrants. Overseers generally blamed the slaves for their precarious economic position, and they were often ruthless toward them. It was not an uncommon practice for angry slaves to drive overseers off plantations because of their cruel treatment, and in many cases overseers were murdered. The following incident, recorded by Botkin, was related by an 80-year-old ex-slave.

> One day when an old woman was plowing in the field, an overseer came by and reprimanded her for being so slow—she gave him some back talk, he took out a long closely woven whip and lashed her severely. The woman became sore and took her hoe and chopped him right across his head, and, child, you should have seen how she chopped this man to a bloody death.

Mobs of angry whites sometimes took it upon themselves to punish slaves accused of serious crimes when they felt that slaveholders were not severe enough in their punishment. Whenever a slave was accused of the murder or rape of a white person, he could expect to be seized by a mob and summarily executed. Some slaves so accused were hanged, but many more were burned to death, frequently in the presence of fellow slaves who were forced to attend these ceremonies.

After attempted slave rebellions, angry whites throughout the slaveholding region assumed responsibility for instilling fear in slaves by a series of acts of violence. They were supported in this behavior by many newspapers, whose editors saw such acts as a means of self-protection. The slaves, on the other hand, frequently found it necessary to resort to violence to dramatize their plight. Acts of violence against slaveholders and their families were commonplace, and they caused a virtual reign of terror by whites in response. Poisoning was one of the methods used by the slaves; others killed their owners by different means. A Kentucky slaveholder, for example, was choked to death by a slave she was flogging. Botkin has recorded one such incident which took place on a plantation in Alabama, as described by a 90-year-old ex-slave.

> The people that owned the plantation near us had lots of slaves. They owned lots of my kinfolks. They master would beat 'em at night when they come from the field and lock 'em up. He'd whup 'em and send 'em to the field. They couldn't visit no slaves, and no slaves was 'lowed to visit 'em. So my cousin Sallie watched him hide the keys. So she moved 'em a little further back so that he had to lean over to reach 'em. That morning soon when he come to let 'em out, she cracked him in the head with the poker and made Little Joe help her

put his head in the fireplace. That day in the field Little Joe made a song: "If you don't believe Aunt Sallie kilt Marse Jim, the blood is on her underdress."

While no exact record of the number of slaveholders killed by their slaves exists, according to John Hope Franklin, such incidents were "exceedingly numerous."

Blacks who were technically free during the era of slavery were, like their fellow blacks who were enslaved, subjected to constant violence and brutality at the hands of whites. As the Civil War approached, so-called "free blacks" were about evenly divided between the cities of the North and South, and in both regions they were frequent targets of mob violence. It was common for roving bands of whites to descend on the black community and terrorize and beat its inhabitants, with little or no provocation. Violence on a wide scale occurred against these black communities in the 1830's and 1840's in New York, Philadelphia, Pittsburgh, Cincinnati and several other cities. During such eruptions the powerless blacks could expect no protection from law enforcement personnel or other public officials.

Violence was an integral part of the relations between blacks and whites. It was deemed necessary by the whites to instill fear in the slaves through force, and the slaves, in responding to this violence, frequently behaved violently themselves. As John Hope Franklin has pointed out in his *The Militant South,* "Violence was inextricably woven into the most fundamental aspects of life in the South and constituted an important phase of the total experience of its people." Given the nature of the institution and the racial attitudes that developed, it is unlikely that slavery could have existed without widespread violence.

Violence continues to be a means of maintaining control over blacks. For hundreds of years slaveholders used acts of brutality as a means of controlling their human property. Blacks who were technically free were nevertheless victims of white mob violence. And with emancipation, after the bloody Civil War, such practices did not cease. Indeed, throughout the Reconstruction period violence and terror were the means regularly used to keep the newly freed ex-slaves from exercising what were felt to be rights reserved for white persons. The sociologist Guy B. Johnson has conservatively estimated that at least 5,000 blacks were killed in the South during Reconstruction by white vigilante groups. Today the forms of violence employed have changed, but the practice itself has persisted.

Lynching

In violence-prone America, lynching became the means by which white citizens protected the community. Consequently, in the early years of America's existence, lynching was a punishment for anyone accused of an offense which outraged the community. Over the years, however, lynching became increasingly a practice reserved for black people, especially black men. It was used as an example of the fate that awaited any black man who challenged white supremacy. During the period when lynching was at its peak it became a practice which was associated almost exclusively with the hanging and burning of blacks.

Data on the incidence of lynching in America are both fragmentary and inadequate. Throughout much of American history no records were kept, and during the period for which records exist the definition of a lynching varied. Nevertheless, since the Civil War thousands of black people have met death at the hands of lynch mobs, regardless of how the term might be defined.

Researchers from Tuskegee Institute have attempted to record the incidence of lynching in the United States since 1882. Based on a rather limited definition, their records distinguish between lynching and murder. The criteria used to establish a lynching contain the following four conditions: 1) there must be legal evidence that a person was killed; 2) the person must have met death illegally; 3) a group must have participated in the killing; 4) the group must have acted under the pretext of service to justice, race or tradition. While such a definition is broader than those used in various attempts to enact federal anti-lynching legislation, it invariably results in an underenumeration of the number of lynchings. For example, in 1964, while dragging the Mississippi River for the bodies of three civil rights workers who had disappeared and who were later discovered to have been murdered, the searchers discovered the mutilated bodies of two black men. It was not known how they met death, and there is every possibility that they were lynched. Rivers, creeks, ponds and fields in many sections of the United States may contain the remains of countless black people who met death at the hands of lynch mobs.

But regardless of the inadequacy of the statistics on lynching, they do give some impression of the extent of violence by white Americans against blacks. It is reported in Tuskegee's *Negro Yearbook* and in the *Negro Almanac* that between 1882 and 1962 a total of 4,736 Americans were lynched. Of this number, 73 percent were black and 27 percent were white. According to these data, an average of 59 Americans were lynched each year during this 80-year period, or more than one a week. For blacks the average was about one every eight days. Lynchings did not occur at a uniform rate, however. During this reporting period blacks were lynched most frequently during the decade of the 1890's, in which period an average of 111 blacks were lynched each year. In the following decade, when the number of whites lynched dropped sharply to an average of nine per year, the lynching of blacks declined to an average of 79 per year.

Reported lynchings of blacks occurred most frequently in the South, which accounted for more than four-fifths of the total in this period. Mississippi led the country in recorded lynchings of black people with a total of 578, followed by Georgia with 491. It is reported that more than 200 black people were lynched in each of the following states: Texas (352), Louisiana (335), Alabama (299), Florida (257), Arkansas (226), and Tennessee (204). The lynching of black people was not limited to the South, however; only the New England states and Arizona, Idaho, Nevada, South Dakota, Wisconsin and the new states of Alaska and Hawaii have no record of blacks having been lynched.

While lynchings have occurred for many reasons, including accusations of homicide, assault and robbery, many black people have been lynched for such "offenses" as "peeping in a window," entering into a dispute with a white man, attempting to vote, violating the racial etiquette of the South, seeking employment in a restaurant, using offensive language, making boastful remarks, and expressing sympathy with a black man who had already been lynched. According to the Southern Commission on the Study of Lynching, alleged rape and charges of attempted rape have been responsible for a significant proportion of the black males lynched. In many cases white women have posed as such victims in order to cover for their own misdeeds, to divert suspicion from a white man, or simply "to have a little excitement." Finally, many cases are recorded in which white rapists have blackened their faces and posed as black men.

In many cases lynchings have been public, often with the cooperation or at least the acquiescence of law enforcement officers. Arrests for lynching black people have been rare, and when participants have been arrested, they have usually not been convicted. In 1947, for example, some 44 persons were indicted for participating in lynchings, but all were freed. And according to Arthur F. Raper, a leading student of lynch mobs, tens of thousands of persons participated in lynch mobs in 1930, but only 49 were indicted and of that number only four were eventually sentenced.

Lynch mobs are said to have been composed primarily of uneducated young males, but Raper presents evidence to show that in many cases they represented a cross section of the communities in which they took place. In addition, the Southern Commission on the Study of Lynching reports that in 1930, a year when twenty black persons and one white man met death at the hands of lynch mobs, these groups included such persons as planters, shopkeepers and religious leaders. Women and children were frequently involved. In one case a grandmother called her two grandsons from bed and took them to see the roasted body of a black man. In another case the wife of a minister is said to have rounded up other spectators, saying "Come, I never did see a nigger burned and I mustn't miss this chance." The major role which women played seems to have been rousing men to action and expressing approval of their actions. According to Raper, they are said to have frequently inspired men to increased brutality. Many lynch mobs have included mothers with children and expectant mothers. Most children were simply observing the excitement, but their presence, like that of women, is said to have incited mobs to greater action and prevented police and other officials from shooting into the crowds.

Participants in lynch mobs have been capable of the most extreme forms of sadism. For example, the Southern Commission on the Study of Lynching reported the case of a black man, James Irwin, who was lynched February 1, 1930, in Ocilla, Georgia, after being accused of rape and murder. He was chased through the night by hundreds of white persons who finally captured him the following morning. He was then taken to the scene of the alleged crime where thousands of eager men, women and children assembled to watch the proceedings. Irwin was hung in a tree by his arms, just high enough to keep his feet off the ground. There, various members of the mob party tortured him for more than an hour. They jabbed a pole in his mouth and cut off his toes, joint by joint. His fingers were removed in the same fashion, and his teeth were extracted with pliers. They then mutilated virtually his entire body and, while he was still alive, saturated his body with gasoline and set him afire. As Irwin burned, hundreds of shots were fired into his body. Throughout the day thousands of spectators traveled many miles to see the sight. It was not until night, when the flow of spectators subsided, that his body was removed by police officers.

In Sherman, Texas, on May 9 of the same year, George Hughes, a black man who had been charged with rape, met a similar fate at the hands of a lynch mob. On the morning of his trial the town was filled with people who made several attempts to take him from the courtroom, but were thwarted by police throwing gasoline bombs. In the early afternoon the courthouse was set afire. Court officials then placed the prisoner in a vault, where he remained while the courthouse burned to the ground, as members of the mob prevented firemen from saving the building. Shortly before midnight some of the mob, using an acetylene torch and explosives, opened the vault and threw Hughes's body to the crowd gathered in the courthouse square. This act was greeted with loud cheers. While the police directed traffic, the corpse was dragged through the streets to the section of town containing businesses owned by blacks. There the corpse was burned to a crisp, along with all the stores owned by blacks.

Raper has described a brutal double lynching. During the night of August 9, 1930, two 19-year-old black men were taken from the jail in Marion, Indiana, and lynched. They had been accused of shooting a white man and raping his companion on August 7. Although the evidence was far from conclusive, when the news reached the white community, talk of lynching the two black men circulated, especially if the white man should die of his gunshot wounds. The white man did die, and a crowd of local white people, estimated between five and six thousand, gathered at the jail where the two blacks were being held.

The sheriff armed his deputies, having been notified by black people that a lynching was imminent, but later decided to take away their guns and rely on a small supply of tear gas to control the mob. Armed with sledge hammers and other weapons, the mob broke open the door to the jail, cheered on by young girls and women with babies in their arms. Upon entering the jail they killed one black man by strangulation. He had apparently attempted to escape through a window, and the members of the mob who waited outside witnessed his death. As he was killed, an 18-year-old white girl was heard to scream, "Hang that nigger!"

The second accused man was taken from the jail to the courthouse square, where his clothes were torn off. He was draped in a large cloth and hanged by the neck from a tree. The mob then brought the body of the black man who had been killed in his cell and hung him beside the other victim. The bodies were left swinging through the night as "object lessons" to the other black people in the town. When the bodies were finally taken down and removed to a neighboring city to be prepared for burial, the local mayor demanded their removal.

One of the most brutal lynchings recorded, in Omaha, Nebraska, on September 29, 1919, has been described by the historian Arthur I. Waskow. A young white girl was said to have been raped and killed, although in fact she was not dead, and her mother identified a black man as her assailant. The man was arrested, and within a short time a mob at the county courthouse demanded that the jailed man be turned over to them. When the mayor of the city refused, he himself was seized by the crowd which attempted to lynch him by hanging him from a trolley pole. The police intervened and temporarily saved his life, but he died the next day from injuries inflicted by the mob.

The crowd, now numbering several thousand, continued to demand that the black man be released to them. They stoned the courthouse. Passing black people, including a policeman, were indiscriminately beaten. By evening a fire was started on the main floor of the building, and when firemen attempted to stop the flames, the firehoses were cut. As the fire spread through the building, the prisoners were forced to the roof. From the roof the black man was thrown to the crowd. The mob shot him, hanged him from a nearby lamp post, then lowered his body and dragged it by the neck for several blocks, during which time members of the crowd kicked the bloody corpse. Finally, the body was hung from a trolley pole and burned. According to one newspaper account, the voices of the crowd, estimated at 10,000, filled "the air with cries of a vengeance fully satisfied." When a wagon arrived for the corpse, the crowd cried, "Let him hang, damn him, let him hang." On the day after the lynching, as much as one-fifth of Omaha's black population of approximately 10,000 fled to Kansas City, St. Louis, and St. Joseph, Missouri. Those who remained armed themselves for self-defense.

Although some were not public, many lynchings of black

people were announced and the public invited to participate. According to accounts and photographs, the crowds often seemed to enjoy these activities. In most cases those who were inactive in the crowd urged the active lynchers on to greater brutality. At the time when lynching was a widespread and frequent practice, a significant proportion of the white people in the South were likely to have observed at least one such act. That they could watch such activities as if they were at a county fair suggests not only the depth of their hatred for blacks, but also the degree to which they lacked qualities normally associated with civilized human beings. That lynchings were so frequent and so well attended indicates the pervasive American disregard for human life.

The economic basis of slavery is clear, and after legal slavery ended the continued oppression of black people served to maintain the economic interests of the ruling class. Poor whites were permitted and encouraged to murder and terrorize poor blacks. Having been robbed of their humanity by the condition of their lives, members of lynch mobs attacked defenseless blacks rather than those responsible for their dehumanization. Although laws were enacted to protect the newly freed blacks, public officials were willing to suspend these laws just as they have been willing to suspend international law in Vietnam.

Race Riots

The lynching of blacks declined in the second decade of the twentieth century. This decline coincided with the massive migration of blacks from the South to other regions of the country, and from rural areas in the South to urban areas within that region. Many who relocated did so in order to escape the anti-black violence which was characteristic of rural areas. But while lynchings were more prevalent in the South, relocation to other sections of the country did not mean that blacks were safe from violence. Elsewhere they became victims of another form of violence—the race riot.

Race riots have occurred throughout the United States, beginning as early as 1829. While they were infrequent prior to the Civil War, they had already occurred in a number of cities, including Cincinnati and New York. During Reconstruction, several major race riots occurred in the South, in cities and in small towns in Louisiana, Mississippi, South Carolina and Tennessee. In Memphis 43 black and two white persons were killed and some 80 persons wounded in rioting in 1866; in the same year 35 persons were killed and more than 100 wounded elsewhere. In Grant Parish, Louisiana, at least 60 blacks were killed in a race riot in 1873, and in 1875 somewhere between 20 and 80 blacks were killed in race riots in other places.

Between 1880 and 1900, years when lynchings were widespread, race riots were rare. During this period most blacks were still in the rural South, and white Southerners had managed to regain their antebellum control. Union troops had been withdrawn, and lynchings and acts of terror were viewed as effective means of containing blacks.

After the turn of the twentieth century, when blacks began to move from the rural South to cities throughout the country, race riots again accelerated. During this period, especially during and immediately after World War I, these riots became widespread, especially outside the South. But the South also had its share of race riots in the early years of the twentieth century: in 1906 major riots occurred in both Atlanta, Georgia, and Brownsville, Texas.

A major riot occurred in East St. Louis, Illinois, on July 2, 1917. At least 39 blacks and eight whites were killed, but no accurate accounting of the deaths exists, and some estimates run as high as 300. This riot resulted from a rumor that a white policeman had been killed by black people. Racial tension had been high in East St. Louis because white workers resented the employment of blacks in a factory with government contracts, and bands of whites had been roaming through the black community indiscriminately shooting into homes. When the rumor spread that the policeman had been killed, whites destroyed the houses in the black community, beating or killing all the blacks they encountered. In one case the mother of a two-year-old child was attacked and the child was shot and thrown into a burning building. Other blacks were tortured while whites looked on approvingly. Police and National Guardsmen either passively observed the activities or participated in them.

As described by sociologist Elliott M. Rudwick and the Chicago Commission on Race Relations, the East St. Louis race riot was one of the most brutal ever recorded. Blacks were outnumbered by about ten to one, and thousands of them fled to nearby cities. The white people who were killed were identified, but most of the blacks killed were never identified.

A race riot in Houston, Texas, in 1917 was responsible for the deaths of 19 people, two blacks and 17 whites. This was one of the few race riots in history where whites suffered greater casualties than blacks, a result no doubt of the fact that the fighting was between black soldiers and white civilians.

The summer of 1919 has been called the "Red Summer" because some 26 major race riots erupted between May and September. Major riots resulting in hundreds of deaths occurred in Charleston, South Carolina; Chicago; Knoxville, Tennessee; Longview, Texas; Omaha; Phillips

County, Arkansas; and Washington, D.C. Of these riots, perhaps the most serious was that in Chicago.

The Chicago race riot, which has been described in detail by Arthur I. Waskow and by the Chicago Commission on Race Relations, lasted from July 27 to August 2. During this time 38 persons were killed (23 blacks and 15 whites), 537 were injured, and at least 1,000 rendered homeless. Race relations in Chicago had been tense because of constant attacks on blacks by gangs of white youths. Five weeks before the riot these gangs had killed two black men in separate, unprovoked attacks. Other attacks continued until Sunday, July 27, when a 17-year-old black youth drowned while swimming in Lake Michigan at 29th Street.

The 29th Street beach had been used by both blacks and whites, with an imaginary line separating the races. The youth had apparently drifted into the water traditionally reserved for white bathers, and when they discovered him, the white bathers threw rocks. A white youth apparently swam near the black youth, at which time he let go of a railroad tie to which he was clinging. The black youth drowned, and word spread among blacks that he had been struck by a rock thrown by a white person. When the blacks insisted that a white man who had been seen throwing rocks be arrested, the police refused. Thereupon the blacks who had gathered mobbed the policeman, and the riot was underway. When police reinforcements arrived, a black man alleged to have fired into a group of police was then killed by a policeman.

The crowd of blacks on the beach attacked all white persons they encountered, and groups of whites attacked all blacks they could find. Between nine P.M. and three A.M. the whites beat 27 blacks, stabbed seven, and shot four. On Monday morning, when blacks employed in the stockyards attempted to go to work, they were beaten by mobs of whites. At street car transfer points, mobs of whites waited for any black person who could be found, who was then either killed or beaten without provocation.

At one point, two injured white people who had been firing at blacks were taken to a black-owned hospital for care. When they heard of this, blacks stabbed six white men, shot five others, and severely beat nine more. Of this number, two died. Elsewhere, a rumor spread that a white occupant in an apartment building had shot a black youth from a window. A crowd of approximately 1500 gathered and demanded that an arrest be made. A flying brick struck a policeman, and the police fired into the crowd, killing four blacks and injuring many more.

The riot spread. Gangs of white men formed, went into black neighborhoods, and terrorized and killed all inhabitants they could find. Others armed themselves with shotguns and revolvers and drove through black neighborhoods firing from automobiles. Blacks resorted to sniping in self-defense. In the center of the city, a group of white sailors in uniform joined others in beating all blacks they encountered. Street cars were stopped, and any black person found was either beaten or killed.

No black gangs were reported to have been involved in vigilante action, but white gangs were reported to have been well organized. It is the opinion of the Chicago Commission on Race Relations that the disturbance would not have developed into a full-scale riot if the white gangs had not been active. Furthermore, it was alleged that many of the fires which destroyed the homes of whites near the stockyards were set by members of these gangs who had painted their faces black. Local newspapers are said to have spread false information about black violence.

The riot atmosphere lasted a total of 13 days, but few deaths or injuries were reported after the first seven days. The police, along with federal troops, were ultimately able to control the acts of violence. As usual, few convictions resulted—in this case, four. The police are said to have been sympathetic to the activities of the white gangs, which led to few apprehensions among them, while many deaths and injuries to black people were attributed to policemen. More black deaths resulted from violence by white mobs than from the police, however. As an example of how one man met death at the hands of a mob, on July 29 a black man died from bullet wounds, stab wounds and a skull fracture. He was returning home from work on a bicycle when he passed through a neighborhood inhabited by Italian-Americans. A rumor spread that a little Italian-American girl had been shot by blacks earlier in the evening, and when the black man was sighted, a mob gathered. He tried to escape by running down an alley and hiding in a basement, but the mob found him, dragged him out, beat and stabbed him and riddled his body with bullets.

Despite the fact that the blacks assembled on the Lake Michigan beach had attacked whites indiscriminately, the Chicago riot followed in general the typical pattern in which whites attacked blacks without provocation. Because the blacks were vastly outnumbered and because the police openly sympathized with and frequently aided the white mob, it was difficult for Chicago's blacks to protect themselves.

Two years later, in 1921, the one major race riot of the 1920's erupted in Tulsa, Oklahoma, when blacks armed themselves and went to the courthouse to prevent the lynching of a black man accused of having assaulted a young white woman. Outbursts of violence spread from the courthouse throughout the city and it is reported that between 21 and 60 blacks, and between nine and 21 whites, were killed before the National Guard could restore order.

The most violent race riot of the 1930's occurred in New York City in 1935. A black youth was accused of stealing a small knife from the counter of a store on 125th Street. He escaped unharmed, but the rumor spread that he had been beaten to death. Crowds of blacks gathered and accused the police of brutality and the merchants of discrimination in employment. In the violence which ensued, three black people were killed.

In the 1940's, while black servicemen were fighting the Germans in Europe and Africa and the Japanese in Asia in a war characterized by the President as one for freedom, their families at home were defending themselves from white violence in the streets, as had been the situation during World War I. During this decade race riots erupted in Detroit, New York, Philadelphia, Athens, Alabama and Columbia, Tennessee. In the Detroit riot, a total of 34 persons were killed (25 blacks and 9 whites), and thousands seriously injured. According to the sociologists Alfred M. Lee and Norman Humphrey, and the writers Robert Shogan and Tom Craig, this riot erupted at a public amusement park when black and white youths engaged in minor scuffles. For at least a week the city of Detroit was a major battleground, with blacks attacking whites indiscriminately and whites attacking blacks without provocation. The Detroit riot of 1943 resembled the Chicago riot of 1919 in that most of its victims were black, and the police either openly sided with the mobs of whites or remained aloof as blacks were beaten or killed.

While major race riots ended in the decade of the 1940's, blacks continued to be victims of violence from whites on a wide scale. With increasing demands for greater civil rights in the 1950's and early 1960's, cities throughout the country became battlegrounds in which thousands of blacks were either beaten or killed by whites. Rarely were they protected from attacks by policemen or others called to maintain order; in many cases the police joined the mobs.

Since the rise of black nationalism in the second half of the 1960's, signaled by the transformation of the civil rights movement into the black liberation movement, hundreds of blacks have been killed and thousands injured in black uprisings, beginning in Los Angeles in 1965. The slaughter of black youths by policemen appears to have been accelerated by their increasing demands for freedom and self-determination.

Race riots, like lynchings, dramatized the division established between poor blacks and poor whites. The people who participated in race riots had been so victimized by a racist, exploitative society that they were blind to the real source of their frustrations: an economic system in which they were at the bottom.

Red People

Unlike the black people, who were brought to what is now the United States beginning early in the seventeenth century, red people had already been long-time inhabitants of this area when the first Europeans appeared. White Americans have conventionally been taught that either Christopher Columbus or Leif Ericson "discovered" America, but it has been estimated that Indians lived in North America anywhere from 12,000 to 35,000 years before the first European settlement. Since the arrival of Europeans, the history of the Indians has been tragic; until 1924 they were even denied citizenship. Furthermore, red people have been subjected to massacres, slavery, disease, kidnapping, expulsion, conquest and forced assimilation, all of which have led to the extermination of complete tribes and the decimation of others.

The exact number of Indian inhabitants of what is now the United States, at the time of European settlement, is not known. Most estimates of aboriginal Indian population put the number at around a million. By the turn of the twentieth century, however, their population had been reduced to less than one-third that number. This population reduction resulted from many factors, not the least of which was a calculated policy of extermination.

When the white man arrived, there were more than 600 Indian tribal societies in what is now the United States, and according to the anthropologist John Collier, these societies "existed in perfect ecological balance with the forest, the plain, the desert, the waters, and the animal life." Warfare between tribal societies was not unknown prior to the arrival of Europeans, but such warfare as existed was of a limited nature. As Collier reports, Indian warfare had been characterized by caution and moderation, which served to maintain population balance and insure tribal continuance. Warfare was rarely waged for the purpose of expansion. With the invasion of the Europeans and their determination to conquer new territory, however, Indian warfare increased in both scope and intensity; warfare became essential for their survival.

For the early settlers, red people impeded "economic progress"; they were on the land and the land had to be settled by people who wanted to make money from it. The Indians were seen as savage beasts who stood in the way of progress. Although treaties were made with them, the treaties were ignored or violated to serve the economic interests of the settlers. Overall, the treatment of Indians in North

America by European settlers stands as one of the most revolting series of acts of violence in human history.

Early Eastern Massacres

When Europeans first arrived in North America, Indians inhabited or used virtually all of the territory from the Atlantic to the Pacific oceans. With white westward expansion, Indians were massacred throughout the land they had known for thousands of years. Although the most widely publicized massacres took place in the nineteenth century, they began with the first European settlement in the seventeenth century. The Christian Pilgrims were in fact the first to massacre Indians and the first to establish a calculated policy of Indian extermination.

The New England coastal area was densely populated with Indians, Algonquian speakers, at the time of European settlement. The Mohegan lived in Connecticut, the Narraganset in Rhode Island, and the Wampanoag and Massachuset lived in what is now Massachusetts. Some seven years after the founding of Plymouth thousands of settlers invaded the region in which these Indians lived. These "Pilgrims" were a land-hungry people, and their relations with the Indians were hardly as friendly as history books have traditionally portrayed them. When in 1616 a smallpox epidemic reduced the Massachuset population from 10,000 to 1,000, these religious colonists rejoiced that the epidemic had, as the historian William Brandon reports, "cleared so many heathen from the path of the Chosen People." But a sufficient number of Indians remained to pose problems for the aggressive settlers, and in 1636 the Massachusetts Bay Puritans sent a force to destroy the Pequot, a division of the Mohegan. The Puritans proceeded to massacre a Pequot village without provocation. Although the Pequot had not attacked the English, they were a powerful people and were considered to be a threat to the colonists.

Taking advantage of the fact that the various Indian tribes had been at war with each other prior to the arrival of Europeans, an English army consisting of 240 colonists, 1,000 Narragansets and 70 Mohegans attacked a Pequot town near the Mystic River in Connecticut, burned all dwellings and slaughtered its 600 inhabitants. After this act the Christian Pilgrims captured and killed the remaining adult males, sold the boys to the West Indies and gave the surviving women and girls to the colonists as slaves. This massacre nearly destroyed the Pequot, and united the New England colonies in their drive against the Indians.

Meanwhile, in 1642 in the Dutch colony of New Netherlands, the governor was offering bounties for Indian scalps. In that year the Wappinger Indians killed a Dutch farmer who had earlier put to death an Indian woman for stealing fruit. The following year, according to Brandon, the drunken Dutch governor ordered the massacre of Wappinger people while they slept. He ordered an army of bloodthirsty men into a village where they murdered 80 Indians and took 30 prisoners. The heads of those murdered were brought back to Manhattan as trophies, where a wealthy white woman is said to have played kickball with them in the street.

During the massacre infants were taken from their mothers' breasts, cut in pieces and thrown into a fire or into the river. Some children who were still alive were also thrown into the river, and when their parents attempted to save them they drowned along with their children. When the massacre was over the members of the murder party were congratulated by the grateful governor.

The Wappingers responded to this act of mass murder by

declaring war on the settlers, whereupon their villages were systematically destroyed. Within a year, some 1,500 had been killed, leaving only 3,500 survivors. Unhappy that some Wappingers had managed to survive, the governor requested permission from the Dutch West India Company to exterminate the remaining Indians. But fearful that such a policy would interfere with business, the directors of the company denied the request, and a precarious peace between the Indians and the settlers was maintained for about 30 years.

During this interval Brandon estimates that the population of European settlers increased to some 50,000, while the total remaining Indian population in the area was estimated at about 20,000. English missionaries were busy converting the Indian "heathens" to Christianity and establishing villages of "praying Indians." But as the population of settlers grew, so did their strength and their desire for land. The proprietors of the colony embarked on a campaign to subjugate the Wampanoag, threatening war if they refused to submit. The son of a Wampanoag chief who was called "King Philip" by the English was forced to submit to the wishes of the colonists in 1671, committing the tribe to pay Plymouth Colony a fixed sum each year.

Relations between the Indians and the settlers worsened, and by 1675 a devastating war erupted. The Indians joined forces against the colonists, but they were outnumbered. Furthermore, the leader of a splinter faction of the Pequot allied his group of 500 warriors with the English, and the praying Indians remained loyal to the missionaries. King Philip, a skillful warrior, commanded the Indian forces, and during the first months of the war the outcome appeared doubtful.

The Indian braves proved to be expert fighters. They attacked more than half of New England's 90 towns, destroying 12 or 13, and killed some 600 colonists. Angered by these successes, the settlers embarked on a campaign to exterminate the Indians. With the death of King Philip in the decisive battle of the war in 1676, the defeat of the Indians became inevitable. When the war was over, surviving Indians were sold into slavery. King Philip's wife and son were held in a prison in Plymouth where his head, along with those of others killed, was displayed on a pole. The clergy of the colony were charged with deciding the fate of King Philip's wife, son and grandson. They voted that the son should be killed, while the wife and grandson should be sold as slaves.

The Algonquian peoples to the North in Maine and Canada suffered widespread starvation after New England's bloodiest war, and other Indians throughout the East fell victim to acts of cruelty from European settlers. Helen Hunt Jackson has described the Conestoga massacre in Pennsylvania in 1763. The Delaware Indians, also an Algonquian people, welcomed the first English settlers in Pennsylvania and entered into a treaty of friendship with William Penn, which was to remain in force "as long as the sun should shine or the waters run into the rivers." And in 1705 the governor of the colony sent a delegation to the Delaware to reaffirm confidence and mutual understanding between them and the colonists. The Indians were impressed with the Quakers because, unlike other settlers, they interacted with them on a basis of friendship and honesty. After the delegation returned, the governor himself went to visit with the Indians to preserve the goodwill which had been established. This was the first of several friendly meetings between the Delaware and governors of the colony.

By 1763 there were only 20 Indians left at Conestoga—seven men, five women and eight children. They were a peaceful but poor people, earning a living by making baskets, brooms, and wooden bowls. On December 14, a band of white men attacked their village. They found only six Indians at home, the other 14 either away working for white farmers or selling their wares. The raiding party killed the three men, two women and a small boy. All were scalped, and the entire village was burned to the ground. The members of the murder party were unknown to the settlers who lived near the Indians.

Outraged by this unprovoked attack, local magistrates rounded up the remaining 14 Indians and brought them to the town jail for protection. The governor of Pennsylvania issued a proclamation ordering law enforcement personnel to apprehend the band of murderers. But two weeks later the murderers, who were known as the "Paxton Boys," rode to the town, entered the jail and killed the remaining Indians. The Indians realized they were defenseless, fell to their knees, pleaded for mercy, and declared their love for the English. They were murdered while on their knees. In this manner the Indians of Conestoga were exterminated.

The governor offered a reward for the apprehension of the murderers, who responded by threatening to attack Quakers and all others sympathetic to the Indians. Furthermore, they announced their intention to completely exterminate the Delaware Indians, who had been placed under the protection of the military. Their actions were defended by clergymen of the day, citing the "Word of God" as justification for destroying "heathens." It thus became dangerous for the Delaware to be seen anywhere.

Quaker missionaries rounded up the Indians, and the governor, realizing that he was powerless to protect them, ordered them relocated to Province Island in the Delaware River. Upon their arrival there the Paxton Boys announced that they planned to march to the island and exterminate them. The governor responded by ordering the Indians north to New York for protection by the English army. But the operator of the ferry, after having been threatened by the mob, refused to transport them. The governor then ordered them back to Philadelphia, where they were housed in army barracks and protected by armed Quaker missionaries. During their stay in the barracks a smallpox epidemic broke out, killing 56 of them.

Hatred of the Indians was so intense among the white settlers who occupied territory surrounding their homeland that it was impossible for the Delaware to return. It was decided they should be relocated to territory along the Susquehanna River. This journey, their third in 18 months, proved to be extremely difficult. Many died along the way, and they were frequently forced to re-route themselves in order to avoid territory occupied by hostile whites. Upon arrival in their new homeland, those who survived the hazardous journey named their village Friedenshutten—"Tents of Peace."

In addition to their East Coast homeland, Delaware Indians lived in villages along the Muskingum River in Ohio. There they were surrounded by tribes of hostile Indians who, in collaboration with the English, forced them to flee northward in 1779 to the Sandusky River. The English suspected that the Delaware had been sympathetic to the colonies during the Revolutionary War, and although they had not participated in the war, the Delaware consented to the move, escorted by hostile Indians led by English officers and accompanied by white missionaries.

The journey, covering more than 100 miles, took one month, and upon their arrival the Delaware built huts to shelter themselves from the winter weather. The white missionaries who remained with them were summoned by the commander of an English fort to answer allegations that the Delaware had aided the colonies during the war. After the meeting he was satisfied that the reports were false and permitted the Indians to settle along the Sandusky River. But the winter was harsh and many of them died from cold and starvation. In the meantime, crops which they had planted home on the banks of the Muskingum River remained ungathered in the fields. Representatives of the tribe decided to return for the food, and on the way they met some missionaries who assured them that they could return permanently to their deserted villages. When they arrived they gathered the crops, stored some grain, and prepared to take the remainder to their starving relatives and friends in Sandusky.

On the day they had planned to return with the foodstuffs, a group of 200 white people appeared in the fields. They welcomed the Delaware back, represented themselves as friends, and offered to take them to a place in Pennsylvania where they would be safe from hostile Indians and the English. According to Jackson, the Indians agreed to make the trip, believing the whites were sincere.

Delaware Indians from nearby villages also were rounded up and prepared for the trip to Pittsburgh. Suddenly all the Indians were attacked, bound with ropes, and confined. The whites held a meeting and decided by a majority of votes that the Delaware should all be killed. Disagreement centered on the method of putting them to death—some favored burning alive, while others preferred scalping. After some discussion the latter method was agreed upon, and the Indians were led into two houses. There the murderers proceeded to kill 96 Indians—62 adults and 34 children. One member of the mob took a sharp-edged mallet and killed 14 persons, after which he gave the instrument to another murderer, saying, "My arm fails me. Go on in the same way. I think I have done pretty well."

While this massacre of the Delaware Indians was one of the most savage ever recorded, it was not the most sinister.

One of the earliest records of the use of germ warfare occurred in 1763, when war between the Indians and the colonies was raging on the western frontiers of Pennsylvania, Maryland and Virginia. Casualties among the settlers were high, and Indian scalping parties are said to have been active. Although the war was fought against the Confederacy of the Iroquois, only the Senecas and the Cayugas were actively engaged.

His Majesty's armed forces in North America were led by General Jeffrey Amherst, with headquarters in New York. His principal assistant was a Colonel Henry Bouquet, a veteran of many wars in Europe who had been recruited expressly for service against the Indians, and who served as commander of the first batallion, with headquarters in Philadelphia. A major military installation of the colonies was Fort Pitt in western Pennsylvania, commanded by Captain Simeon Ecuyer.

Amherst ordered that no prisoners be taken and that any Indians captured "immediately be put to death, their extirpation being the only security of our future safety, and their treacherous proceedings deserving no better treatment from our hands." After a captain had been killed by the Senecas in July, all officers leading troops were instructed by Amherst to treat Indians "not as a generous enemy, but as the vilest race of beings that ever infested the earth, and whose riddance from it must be esteemed a meritorious act, for the good of mankind."

Francis Parkman and Howard Peckham, historians of the wars against the Indians, have reprinted correspondence between Amherst and Boquet in which a plan was devised, after several military defeats, to use germ warfare against the Indians. In a letter to Boquet, Amherst made the following suggestion: "Could it not be contrived to send the Small Pox among those disaffected tribes of Indians? We must on this occasion use every stratagem in our power to reduce them."

Boquet replied: "I will try to inoculate the —— with some blankets that may fall in their hands, and take care not to get the disease myself. As it is a pity to expose good men against them, I wish we could make use of the Spanish method, to hunt them with English dogs, supported by rangers and some light horses, who would, I think, effectively extirpate or remove that vermin."

Amherst rejoined: "You will do well to try to inoculate the Indians by means of blankets, as well as to try every other method that can serve to extirpate this execrable race. I should be very glad if your scheme for hunting them down with dogs could take effect, but England is at too great a distance to think of that at present."

Although there is no written evidence that Boquet put the plan of infecting the Indians with smallpox into effect, a few months later smallpox did rage among the Indians in the area, killing hundreds of them. In addition, there is evidence that Captain Ecuyer employed this device against the Indians. On one occasion, for example, he invited several Indian chiefs to a peace conference, and after both sides concurred on the terms of the peace agreement, Ecuyer gave the chiefs a present of two blankets and a handkerchief, all of which had been infected in the smallpox hospital at Fort Pitt. A white man who was captured by the Indians and later released reported that smallpox had decimated them.

The Trail of Tears

One of the most brutal of all acts perpetrated against Indians by whites involved the Cherokees in the Southeast. The first contact between these people and Europeans had occurred as early as 1540 when DeSoto passed through their homeland. This contact with Spanish explorers was brief and generally unpleasant, and the Cherokees expressed the hope that it would be the end of contact with Europeans. But a century and a half later more white people appeared, this time the British. Since these newcomers, unlike the Spanish, did not come as explorers, but gave every indication of settling in the region, the Indians greeted them in friendship.

The Cherokees were a proud and powerful people, the largest of the Iroquoian tribes, with an eastern homeland situated in what are now the states of Alabama, Georgia, North Carolina and Tennessee. In a series of negotiations with Great Britain, several treaties were signed and there were repeated manifestations that the newcomers desired to live in peace with the Indians. In 1734, for example, a delegation of eight Indian chiefs was invited to England by King George, where they were also received by the Archbishop of Canterbury and by the Fellows of Eton, and were entertained for four months. The reasons for this hospitality were to pave the way for English settlement in the region and to convert the Indians to Christianity.

Although the first English settlers to arrive in the Georgia colony were dishonest in their relations with the Indians, the Cherokees were eager to live in peace with them. The Indians were impressed with the skills the settlers brought with them, but a series of wars erupted, massacres were common, and treaties were broken. However, a treaty was concluded in 1763 in which the Cherokees granted the King of England a large tract of land, and both sides honored its terms for several years.

Because of their relations with the British Government, the Cherokees remained loyal to England during the Revolutionary War, except for a small number of them who fought on the side of the colonies. With independence, the Government of the United States moved to conquer the tribe and confiscate their lands. The Hopewell Treaty of 1785 declared that the officials of the new government "want none of your lands, nor anything else which belongs to you," although most of the Cherokees had been "enemies" assisting "the King of Great Britain in his endeavors to conquer our country." The Cherokee chiefs then requested that the vast sections of their land which had been occupied by settlers be vacated. Their request was rejected, but they were given token payment for the land. The new settlers continued to demand land from the Indians, and in 1791 the Holston Treaty was ratified between the Cherokees and the Government of the United States, establishing new boundaries for Cherokee lands and declaring that "if any citizen of the United States or other person (not an Indian) shall settle on the Cherokee's lands, the Cherokees may punish him as they please."

As relations between the Cherokees and white settlers deteriorated, it was necessary in 1794 to make still another treaty, primarily to declare that the Holston Treaty was still in force. But attacks on Indians and confiscation of their lands continued. Several states attempted to pacify the Indians by paying for the confiscated lands, but the Cherokees were more interested in retaining their homeland. By 1828 their land had been reduced to a small fraction of its original size.

With the election of Andrew Jackson as President in this year, relations between the Cherokees and whites reached their nadir. Jackson had been a famous Indian fighter, and one of his first acts as President was to push through Congress the Indian Removal Act, which gave him responsibility for removing all Indians to some area west of the Mississippi River. At about the same time, as Collier reports, gold was discovered in Cherokee country, and the Georgia Legislature responded to this discovery by passing a law confiscating all Cherokee lands within the state. This legislation, enacted in December 1829, declared "all laws, ordinances, orders, and regulations of any kind whatever, made, passed, or enacted by the Cherokee Indians, either in general council or in any other way whatever, or by any authority whatever, null and void, and of no effect, as if the same had never existed." It also decreed "that no Indian, or descendant of any Indian residing within the Creek or Cherokee nations, shall be deemed a competent witness in any court of this State to which a white man may be a party."

In 1830 the Cherokee chief appealed in vain to President Jackson. An appeal was then directed to the Supreme Court, but the Court refused to take jurisdiction on the grounds that the Cherokees did not constitute a separate nation. Two years later, however, the Court reversed itself, ruling that "the Cherokee nation . . . is a distinct community, occupying its own territory, with boundaries accurately described, in which the laws of Georgia can have no force, and which the citizens of Georgia have no right to enter, but with the assent of the Cherokees themselves, or in conformity with treaties, and with the acts of Congress." This decision was cause for celebration among the Cherokees, but of it President Jackson said: "[Chief Justice] John Marshall has rendered his decision; now let him enforce it."

Because of the refusal of the President to execute the decision of the Court, a reign of terror befell the Cherokees. Military law was imposed in Georgia, Cherokees were executed without cause, their land was distributed to whites in lotteries, they were forbidden to prospect for gold while whites could do so anywhere, and missionaries were arrested for preaching to them. The response of the Cherokees was to petition the Supreme Court, requesting that the State of Georgia be restrained from interfering with their rights. This time a majority of the justices ruled that the Cherokees did not constitute a foreign nation and therefore could not bring the suit.

The President appointed a commission which met with 400 of the tribe's 17,000 members, and forced them to sign a treaty giving up the remaining 7,000,000 acres of Cherokee land for $4,500,000, to be deposited to their credit in the United States Treasury. The Cherokees refused to honor this treaty, which had been negotiated by persons who did not represent them, and remained on their land. Within a few years, some 7,000 troops, led by General Winfield Scott and accompanied by white settlers eager to seize Indian land, invaded Cherokee territory. Cherokee men, women and children were rounded up at gun point and forced into concentration camps. Their homes were burned, and graves were opened for the silver and other valuables they had buried with their dead.

From the concentration camps the Cherokees were forced to march on foot to territory west of the Mississippi River. Of the 14,000 who made the journey, some 4,000 died on the way in what has come to be known as "the trail of tears." Collier estimates that 100 Cherokees a day perished from the cold and exhaustion during the forced march. In a message to Congress on December 3, 1838, President Van Buren reported that "The measures authorized by Congress at its last session have had the happiest of effects . . . The Cherokees have emigrated without any apparent reluctance." As a final act of cruelty, the financial costs of the removal were charged against the funds held for the Cherokees in the Treasury Department.

The official position of the federal government toward the Cherokees and toward Indians in general was succinctly stated in 1871 by General Francis C. Walker, Commissioner of Indian Affairs: "When dealing with savage beasts, no question of national honor can arise. Whether to fight, to run away, or to employ a ruse, is solely a question of expediency." It is a grim irony that the Cherokees were unable to find peace even in their new homeland, where land-hungry whites continued to rob them of the territory they inhabited. Yet the Cherokees have succeeded in purchasing back about one percent of their original land. And during World War II, approximately 17 percent of the Cherokee population in the East served in the armed forces, fighting on every front and suffering heavy casualties, all in the service of a country which annihilated most of their ancestors and which still refuses to accord them the status of human beings.

Nineteenth Century Western Massacres

As the European settlers and their descendants moved west in the middle of the nineteenth century, they encountered the Plains Indians. In the first half of the century the Plains Indians were considered an exciting and romantic people, posing no threat to the settlers who visited in the region. But the discovery of gold and the desire for economic expansion changed these notions. Suddenly the Indians became treacherous savages, impeding the progress of the civilized white people.

Among the most populous Indian tribes on the plains were the Cheyenne, an Algonquian-speaking people, who had been pushed from Minnesota west into what is now Colorado by the Sioux around 1700. In Minnesota they had been farmers, but in the new territory they obtained horses and became hunters. The tribe divided in 1832, some going to the south and others remaining in the north, and the division became permanent by treaty with the United States in 1851. As the settlers pushed west across the plains, they encountered hostility from the Cheyenne because they drove the buffalo herds from their hunting grounds. Whenever friction erupted, the settlers called upon troops to protect them.

The Plains Indians engaged in frequent warfare with the settlers because of attempts to confiscate their lands, and in 1862 they staged an uprising during which many settlers were massacred. Troops were finally summoned, and the Indians were defeated. During this time most of the soldiers in the Army of the United States were engaged in the Civil War; consequently, volunteer troops were dispatched to contain the Indians. The volunteer troops engaged in skirmishes with the Southern Cheyennes until October 1864, when the Indians indicated that they wanted peace. The Cheyenne peace party met with the Governor of Colorado and the commander of a nearby military installation, who urged them to establish a village at Sand Creek, 30 miles from Fort Lyon.

The Colorado volunteer militia was headed by the Reverend J. M. Chivington, a colonel, who had earlier attacked the Cheyenne because of a false report that they had stolen cattle from a government contractor. By the end of November, when the Indians settled at Sand Creek, Colonel Chivington ordered a force of nearly 1,000 volunteers to attack the village, saying: "Kill and scalp all big and little; nits make lice." The volunteers enthusiastically carried out the order, killing at least 300 and possibly as many as 500 Indians, mostly women and children. After the massacre Chivington sent a victory message back to Denver: "I at daylight this morning attacked a Cheyenne village of . . . from nine hundred to a thousand warriors. We killed . . . between four and five hundred. All did nobly."

Ralph K. Andrist has vividly described the Sand Creek massacre. A woman leaving a tepee was the first to discover the volunteers on a bluff. When she shouted an alarm, Black Kettle, the leading chief of the Cheyenne and a man of peace, raised an American flag, which was met by a blast of cannon and rifle fire. There were few weapons among the Indians, and they were soon overpowered. When women and children pleaded to be spared, the Colorado volunteers slaughtered them at close range. A pregnant woman was cut open and her unborn child removed from her womb. White Antelope, an old chief of 70, was killed and his genitals removed by a soldier who declared he would make a tobacco pouch of them. Mothers were killed with babies in their arms.

Nine people were taken captive—two men, three women and four children. They were taken to Denver along with the scalps of dozens of other Indians and exhibited at a theater, where Chivington and his band of murderers provided running commentary as they displayed their terrified captives and the scalps of their victims. The audience roared its approval.

Later, however, in response to growing public outrage at the Sand Creek massacre, a military commission was appointed to investigate. Most of the witnesses who appeared had been present at Sand Creek, and most of them testified against Chivington, who had resigned his commission to avoid a court-martial. One officer, a captain, testified that he had been unwilling to participate in the bloodbath and had refused to order his men to fire on the village. As a result of this testimony, he became a target of physical attack by angry settlers and was ultimately killed.

Congress agreed to pay reparations to the widows and orphans of those murdered at Sand Creek, but the massacre had served to unify the Plains Indians, who sought revenge. They attacked wagon trains and villages, and killed settlers. Even new detachments of troops were unable to stop the Indians, and the government decided to starve them by burning the land they used for grazing and driving all game from the region. Millions of acres of land were devastated, and the Indians fled to new territory.

By 1868 Black Kettle and his people had settled on the banks of the Washita River in Oklahoma. In the winter of that year his village was the target of an unexpected attack by soldiers who had been ordered to destroy the village and kill every male Indian over 12 years of age. The troop commander was Lieutenant Colonel George A. Custer, and the attack was his first major engagement with the Indians. His men killed more than 140 men, women and children, including Black Kettle.

Wars against the Indians intensified after the discovery of gold in the Black Hills in 1874, and a campaign was launched to recruit fighters among local residents, with a bounty of $100 for each Indian scalp. The most powerful of the Plains Indians left were the Sioux, and their warriors were commanded by Crazy Horse and Sitting Buffalo, also known as Sitting Bull. The Black Hills region had been guaranteed to the Sioux by treaty, but after the discovery of gold attempts were made to take it from them. In 1876, the year of the first centennial of the United States, an army of 1,000 troops attacked the main body of Sioux, who had refused to give up the Black Hills land. This battle was fought in southern Montana, and when the troops withdrew to await reinforcements the Indians moved to another river to establish a camp. One week later their new village was attacked by the Seventh Cavalry, led by Custer. Both Crazy Horse and Sitting Bull led the Indians in repelling the attack and dividing the cavalrymen into two groups. One group was surrounded, and in less than half an hour the Indians killed all 260 of them, including Custer. The news of this humiliating defeat was reported in Eastern newspapers the morning of July 5, in the midst of centennial ceremonies, and cries of revenge spread throughout the country. Having no means of sustaining a standing army, the Indians split into small bands and were subsequently either captured and forced onto reservations or driven north into Canada.

But peace had not come to the plains. During the grim years when the Indians who remained were being decimated by disease and starvation, a messiah suddenly appeared, giving birth to a religion that became known to whites as the Ghost Dance. The messiah preached that the ghosts of dead Indians were available to help their survivors in time of need, and the cult quickly spread among the Plains Indians, terrifying white settlers who thought that it would lead to uprisings. Consequently, practitioners of the Ghost Dance were systematically arrested. Sitting Bull was killed in the process of being taken prisoner.

Shortly after Christmas in 1890, more than 300 Sioux, mainly women and children, were forced into a camp on Wounded Knee Creek in South Dakota and arrested by a unit of the Seventh Cavalry. They were surrounded by 500 cavalrymen, with four rapid-fire Hotchkiss guns pointed directly at their camp. The Sioux raised a white flag and all the warriors left their tepees, sitting on the ground in a semicircle. They were instructed to return to their tents to collect their weapons, and when they returned with only two guns, enlisted men were ordered to search for additional weapons. In the midst of the search, a medicine man walked among the Indians blowing an eagle-bone whistle and urging them to resist, since the Ghost shirts they wore made them invulnerable to bullets. An Indian warrior who had hidden his gun under his blanket suddenly pulled it out and fired into the line of soldiers, killing one of them. The troops responded by firing on the warriors, and the surviving Sioux men threw off their blankets and charged the soldiers with their hands. At the same time the Hotchkiss guns opened fire on the women and children in the tepees.

The other troops joined in firing on the women and children, who were slaughtered as they attempted to flee. Once the firing ceased, according to Andrist, the line of bodies of dead women and children extended more than two miles from the camp. The number of Indians killed in the massacre of Wounded Knee has been put at 300, two-thirds of them women and children. The frozen dead were gathered in wagons and buried in a common grave on New Year's Day, 1891.

Black Elk, a holy man of the Sioux who lived across the hills from Wounded Knee, described the massacre to John G. Neihardt in 1930. He reported what he had seen after his party arrived at Wounded Knee:

> By now other Lakotas, who had heard the shooting, were coming up from Pine Ridge, and we all charged on the soldiers. They ran eastward toward where the trouble began. We followed down along the dry gulch, and what we saw was terrible. Dead and wounded women and children and little babies were scattered all along there where they had been trying to run away. The soldiers had followed along the gulch, as they ran, and murdered them in there. Sometimes they were in heaps because they had huddled together, and some were scattered all along. Sometimes bunches of them had been

> killed and torn to pieces where the wagon guns hit them. I saw a little baby trying to suck its mother, but she was bloody and dead.

The massacre of Wounded Knee was the end of the major wars between the Plains Indians and the soldiers of the United States. It was also the end of the Ghost Dance as a religion among the Sioux. But it was not the end of the settlers' greediness, for the Plains Indians have since lost three-fifths of the land they possessed at the time of the massacre. They have only the worthless land set aside for them by the white people who invaded their homeland and did their best to exterminate them.

In the early years of nationhood, blacks were killed selectively, since they represented important economic investments, but Indians were viewed as savage beasts to be exterminated because they impeded economic progress. Hence milder forms of violence were usually directed at blacks. With the end of slavery, however, blacks met the brutality Americans have usually reserved for people of different races, both at home and overseas. Acts of violence against blacks have continued to the present time because blacks are seen as threatening, while Indians have been somewhat spared because of their confinement to inaccessible reservations.

The United States has a long history of aggressive violence by white persons against those of different races, dating back to the beginnings of European settlement in North America. And just as the army could be relied on to massacre slaves attempting to revolt in the antebellum period, to massacre Indians for nearly three centuries and guerrillas in the Philippines in the early twentieth century, today they slaughter peasants in Indochina and blacks at home to maintain the status quo of power and privilege. Indeed, the descendants of those who killed at the Pequot and Wounded Knee massacres are among the people who massacre in Mylai 4 and Detroit. In a bizarre turn of events they have been joined in their violent acts by the dehumanized descendants of the peoples they slaughtered.

V

▶▶▶▶▶▶

Police Violence

The Law Enforcement Code of Ethics binds policemen to the following: "I will never act officiously or permit personal feelings, prejudices, animosities or friendships to influence my decisions. With no compromise for crime and with relentless prosecution of criminals, I will enforce the law courteously and appropriately without fear or favor, malice or ill will, never employing unnecessary force or violence and never accepting gratuities." Punishment is not a police function, but rather the responsibility of the courts. Yet throughout much of American history the police have been accused by citizens of punishing them through the excessive use of force.

While police brutality may take many forms, such as physical assault, the use of unnecessary force or abusive language, it is usually unnecessary physical violence which has formed the basis of recent studies of police abuse of power. The police and other law enforcement personnel in the United States have historically used their positions to legitimize violence against members of ethnic minorities, labor organizers and strikers, political dissenters and other non-conformists. In recent years, however, charges of police brutality have led to a degree of public concern without parallel in American history. Citizens in cities throughout the country, usually members of ethnic minorities, have demanded the creation of civilian review boards to hear complaints of police misconduct. Police departments and organizations representing the interests of policemen have invariably opposed these proposals. Recently, black and other minority group spokesmen have demanded that large city police departments be decentralized and that the police serving in local communities be held responsible to the residents of these communities. In some nonwhite communities, such as the Watts section of Los Angeles and the Mexican-American section of Denver, residents regularly patrol the streets to check on police treatment of nonwhite people. In both instances, the local citizens have been able thereby to curb police violence toward blacks and Mexican-Americans.

Members of ethnic minorities and juveniles frequently meet violence at the hands of the police. This is common knowledge; yet few citizens appear to be concerned about such behavior. Indeed, violence on the part of the police has become institutionalized in the society. As Edgar Friedenberg has written, "Most Americans would say they disapproved of violence. But what they really mean is that they believe it should be a monopoly of the state."

Just as American military forces attempt to maintain the status quo throughout the world, the police maintain the status quo at home. The police are therefore the agents of the ruling class, ruthlessly protecting its interests. In this role they have permitted themselves to be turned against the people, and have gone to any length, including murder, to serve the interests of their employers.

Increasing black militance, opposition to the war in Vietnam and demands for reform in many areas of American life have in recent years brought increasing numbers of citizens into contact with the police. In these encounters, the police have frequently demonstrated that they were willing to commit acts of violence on a wide scale. I have selected the cases in this chapter because they represent examples in which police have been observed committing acts of violence against citizens with minimal or no provocation, resulting either in deaths or serious injuries. As they indicate, the police comprise one segment of the society in which violence against certain categories of citizens is an accepted practice.

Recent Police Violence Against Blacks

Although it has been asserted that white citizens are more likely than blacks to be subjected to police brutality, blacks are more likely than whites to be victims of extreme police violence. Throughout American history thousands of blacks have been killed by white policemen, and with the rise of black nationalism in the 1960's the killings of blacks by police has sharply increased. While these killings have occurred throughout the country, they have recently been centered in large cities outside the South.

According to the report of the National Advisory Commission on Civil Disorders, police practices were cited by residents of black communities which had experienced black uprisings between 1963 and 1967 as their major grievance, surpassing unemployment, substandard housing, inadequate education and similar critical concerns. During the height of the civil rights movement in the South, police violence directed against blacks and their white supporters was widespread. Indeed, police officials were frequently implicated in the killing of civil rights activists; a deputy sheriff in Mississippi, for example, was among those convicted of the murder of three civil rights workers in that state in the summer of 1964. But in recent years urban centers outside the South have become the major centers for confrontations between the police and blacks, often resulting in the killing of blacks.

Members of black nationalist groups are the targets of extreme police violence, and the members of the Black Panther Party appear to be special targets. The Panther Party, founded in Oakland, California, in 1966 to curb police violence against black people, was one of the first organizations in which blacks armed themselves against white violence. Its members publicly declared their willingness to fight back, and openly displayed weapons. In addition, the Party developed an ideological position strongly opposed to capitalism. Marxism-Leninism became its officially stated ideology, stressing class over race. The position of the Party was set forth in a statement released at its headquarters:

> The Black Panther Party stands for revolutionary solidarity with all people fighting against the forces of imperialism, capitalism, racism and fascism. Our solidarity is extended to those people who are fighting these evils at home and abroad. Because we understand that our struggle for liberation is part of a worldwide struggle being waged by the poor and oppressed against imperialism and the world's chief imperialist, the United States of America, we—the Black Panther Party—understand

> that the most effective way that we can aid our Vietnamese brothers and sisters is to destroy imperialism from inside, attack it where it breeds . . . We will take our stand against these evils with a solidarity derived from a proletarian internationalism born out of socialist idealism.

Huey P. Newton, co-founder, Minister of Defense and Supreme Commander of the Black Panther Party, has defined the goals of the Party: "We are attempting to transform an oppressive capitalist society into a socialistic society in which each man shall participate in the decisions that affect his life, thus making him free."

The willingness of the Black Panthers to arm themselves for self-defense and for the defense of the black community, combined with their opposition to the economic system of the United States, has led to a determination by those in power to destroy the organization. High government officials —the President, the Attorney General, the Vice-President, the director of the Federal Bureau of Investigation—have permitted or encouraged the police to murder Panthers throughout the country although they have violated no laws. Indeed, they publicly direct local police to defy the laws of the country in their drive to eliminate the Black Panther Party. And the police are only too willing to serve as agents for the ruling oligarchy.

In 1968 and 1969 alone, at least 28 members of this organization, including many of its national leaders, were killed by the police. Early in the morning of December 4, 1969, fifteen members of the State's Attorney's office of Cook County, armed with submachine guns and shotguns, in addition to regular revolvers, entered an apartment on Chicago's West Side occupied by members of the Black Panther Party. When they left two persons were dead—Fred Hampton, age 21, who served as Chairman of the Illinois chapter of the Party, and Mark Clark, age 22, a Panther leader from Peoria, Illinois. Four other Panthers, including a woman, were wounded. According to the police officials, these deaths resulted from a gun battle between the police, who had secured a search warrant, and the Panthers. However, only two of the police officers involved were injured, one struck on the hand by flying glass and the other grazed by a shotgun pellet on the left leg. All evidence indicates that Hampton was killed while sleeping and that bullets and shotgun pellets traveled only into the bedroom where the Panther officials were sleeping.

Few incidents have caused as much concern in the black community as the deaths which resulted from this pre-dawn, gang-style raid on the members of the Black Panther Party. Eight official and unofficial investigations of the raid were carried out, including one by the Civil Rights Division of the Department of Justice. This latter investigation proved that those who were killed had been murdered without reason by the police. Similar raids have been made on Panther headquarters and offices throughout the country, often simultaneously at several locations. It is for these reasons that Panther leaders insist there is a nationwide conspiracy to destroy their organization. Government officials deny this charge, but FBI Director J. Edgar Hoover has branded the Black Panther Party the "greatest threat to the internal security of the United States." By the end of 1969 most national leaders of the organization had either been killed, jailed or forced into exile.

A brief summary of the major police-Panther clashes in the years 1968–1969 was compiled by the American Civil Liberties Union and published in the *New York Times.* In January 1968, San Francisco police, without a warrant, raided the home of Eldridge Cleaver, Minister of Information of the Black Panther Party. In February Cleaver and his wife were arrested in their home by Oakland police without a warrant. Four other members of the Party were arrested at the same time. Charges against them were ultimately dropped, but only after two of them had been killed by the police. In April Cleaver, another high Panther official and six other members of the Party were charged with attempted murder of two Oakland policemen. The charges were later dropped, but Bobby Hutton, a founder of the Party, was killed in an alleged shoot-out with the police. In September the Denver police arrested three Panthers for allegedly contributing to the delinquent behavior of juveniles. All were later released because of lack of evidence. The Denver police arrested one Panther and killed another for alleged sniping, and the Colorado chairman of the Party was arrested for arson. No evidence was offered, and the charges were ultimately dropped. In November eight Panthers were arrested on charges of shooting at the police in San Francisco. Charges were dropped against seven, but one was later arrested while allegedly robbing a service station. And in December the Panther headquarters in Jersey City was firebombed by two white men "wearing police-style uniforms."

The year 1969 was a more serious one for the Panthers. In April, 21 of them were indicted in New York for conspiracy to blow up the botanical gardens, department stores, etc. Although no overt act was ever charged, and none of the Panthers had a serious police record, bail for the group was set at over two million dollars. During the same month the San Francisco police, using tear gas, raided the headquarters of the Party and arrested 16 persons. Twelve were released with no charges filed, but four were charged with illegal use of sound equipment. In May the Los Angeles police raided Party headquarters, seized weapons and arrested 11 persons, all of whom were later released without charges.

The Chicago police raided the Party headquarters in June and arrested eight persons for harboring a fugitive. No fugitive was found, but the police confiscated money, membership lists and literature. The arrested persons were later released, but the confiscated money and materials were not returned. Also in June, the Detroit police raided a Party office and arrested three persons on a charge of possessing stolen goods. All were later released for lack of evidence. Denver police raided Party headquarters in June and arrested 10 persons on federal warrants charging flight to avoid prosecution. Eight were later released, and no charges were filed. In California the Santa Ana police arrested a Party officer for allegedly shooting a policeman. The charge was later dropped. Police in Sacramento, using tear gas, raided the Party offices in search of an alleged sniper. No sniper was found, but in the raid the Panther offices were totally destroyed.

The Chicago police again raided the Panther headquarters on July 31. This time the building was totally destroyed, and the three persons present were wounded and arrested for attempted murder, aggravated assault and resisting arrest. California police were active against the Panthers in September. In San Diego the police raided Party offices in search of a murder suspect. The suspect was not found, but the police confiscated weapons and ammunition. In Los Angeles a Party member was killed by two policemen who claimed he had fired on them. In December David Hilliard, the only national Panther leader alive and free at the time, was arrested in San Francisco for threatening the life of the President of the United States. Hilliard had said in a public speech, "We will kill Richard Nixon—we will kill *any* motherfucker that stands in the way of our freedom." And in Los Angeles the police raided the headquarters again, this time wounding three persons. A total of 21 persons were arrested in coordinated raids in three locations in the city, including a pregnant woman who suffered a miscarriage.

After these search-and-destroy missions against the Panthers, the police often display caches of weapons. But there are many white vigilante groups (e.g., the Ku Klux Klan and the Minutemen) whose members regularly store arms, and when such groups are raided (which occurs infrequently), their members are not usually killed. Consequently, even more conservative black leaders charge that the killing of members of the Black Panther Party is a coordinated effort to curb increasing black militance.

While the Black Panthers have frequently been involved in violent clashes with the police (which the police invariably assert were initiated by the Panthers), there have been cases in which the police were obviously responsible for the violence directed against unarmed Panthers. Three members of the Brooklyn chapter of the Black Panther Party had been arrested on charges of assaulting police officers and resisting arrest, and a preliminary hearing was held in Brooklyn Criminal Court on September 4, 1968. Panthers and their supporters, including members of the Students for a Democratic Society (SDS) and the Peace and Freedom Party, attended the hearing. Almost all the seats in the courtroom were occupied, but a small group of Panthers, perhaps eight or nine, were permitted to enter the courtroom. The hearing proceeded without incident, but when the Panthers attempted to leave, they were attacked by a group of some 150 off-duty white policemen in the halls of the courthouse. The policemen, wearing "Wallace for President" campaign buttons, attacked the Panthers and their supporters with blackjacks, and kicked them. The clubbing and kicking lasted for several minutes, and the attackers were observed by newsmen as displaying "the characteristic bulge made by a revolver such as is worn by off-duty policemen in a holster on the right hip." After blood was flowing in the hallway of the courthouse, on-duty policemen who had been observing their co-workers in action moved in and escorted the battered group of Panthers and their supporters to an elevator, by which they were permitted to leave the building. No arrests were ever made, although it was acknowledged that the initiators of the violence were off-duty policemen.

Throughout the United States the police openly admit their hostility toward the Panthers. Similarly, the Panthers acknowledge their contempt for the police and their role as occupying forces in the black community. Indeed, the Black Panther Party was first organized as a self-defense organization in the black community. Point seven of its platform states: "We want an immediate end to police brutality and mass murder of black people." It is ironic that the Panthers should fall victim to a condition which they organized to curb.

In spite of the many charges against the Panthers and unfair characterizations by public officials, Jerome Skolnick, director of the task force on group violence of the National Commission on the Causes and Prevention of Violence, was able to write in his final report, *The Politics of Interest:* "'The Black Panther Party has remained defensive, and has been given credit for keeping Oakland cool after the assassination of Martin Luther King, but this has not stemmed from any desire on their part to suppress black protest in the community. Rather, it has stemmed from a sense that the police are waiting for a chance to shoot down blacks in the streets. Continued harassment by the police makes self-defense a necessary element of militant action for the Panthers and for similar groups, such as the Black Liberators in St. Louis."

The Black Panther Party, as an organization of black militants armed to curb police violence against blacks and espousing an ideology opposed to the American economic system, is a logical target of official America. In addition to awakening the political consciousness of black people, the Party has served to educate many white youths to the contradictions in the American system, and of the lengths to which the ruling class and its agents, the police, are willing to go to maintain it.

A highly publicized recent incident of police-initiated violence against blacks, and one which did not directly involve so-called black militants, occurred during the black uprising in Detroit in the summer of 1967. On the fourth day of that uprising, three black youths were killed by Detroit policemen in the Algiers Motel, an episode studied by John Hersey in his book *The Algiers Motel Incident.* The report of the National Advisory Commission on Civil Disorders reported the incident in one brief paragraph: "Prosecution is proceeding in the case of three youths in whose shotgun deaths law enforcement personnel were implicated, following a report that snipers were firing from the Algiers Motel. In fact, there is little evidence that anyone fired from inside the building. Two witnesses say that they had seen a man, standing outside of the motel, fire two shots from a rifle. The interrogation of other persons revealed that law enforcement personnel then shot out one or more street lights. Police patrols responded to the shots. An attack was launched on the motel." But the incident received considerably more publicity, especially in the black community, because it involved a case in which three Detroit policemen, motivated by anti-black prejudice and with the aid of a black private guard, summarily killed three black youths, apparently because they were discovered in a motel room with two white women. Black leaders in Detroit quickly formed a coalition called the Citywide Citizens' Action

Committee, which selected a group of nationally known black people to serve as jurors for a People's Tribunal which tried the policemen, a National Guardsman, and the private guard for the massacre of the three young black men.

Throughout the uprising of July 22 to July 27, 1967, the black people of Detroit engaged in a battle with city and state police, National Guardsmen and United States paratroopers. In the six-day period 43 people were killed, including 33 black and 10 white persons. It is significant that various accounts attribute anywhere from 18 to 21 of the deaths to the police. Some 17 deaths were occasioned by the act of looting, in which individuals may have been guilty of stealing a few dollars' worth of merchandise, but were forced by the police to pay with their lives, for they had violated the sanctity of private property.

But Carl Cooper (17 years old), Aubrey Pollard (19 years old) and Fred Temple (17 years old) were not looters, arsonists or snipers; they were not even active participants in the black uprising in Detroit. They were in the Algiers Motel on the evening of July 24 with seven of their friends and two white women, when state police and National Guardsmen received a report of sniper fire in the vicinity of the motel. These officials entered the building, and when they left, the three black youths were dead, having been beaten and shot at close range, and all the other occupants, including the women, severely beaten. No weapons were found, and there is no evidence that sniper fire emanated from the motel.

The murdered youths, from descriptions of them by parents, siblings, friends and former teachers, appeared to be typical of others in this age group. Cooper was described as a good student in school, one who liked music and dancing. Pollard was interested in art and was said to have won prizes for his drawings, some of which had been exhibited in

Detroit and New York. He enjoyed swimming and served as a lifeguard at the YMCA. Temple, the youngest of seven children, left high school after completing his junior year. He was interested in photography. Cooper had a minor police record and Pollard had been accused of striking a teacher in school, but Temple had no such record, either with the police or with school officials.

The autopsies performed by the Deputy Medical Examiner of the Wayne County Morgue disclosed that they had not only been shot at close range but had been beaten. Cooper died from "multiple shotgun wounds of chest and abdomen with penetrating wounds of lungs, heart, liver, stomach, and aorta." In addition, he suffered "multiple compound comminuted fractures of the left upper arm." Pollard died of a "shotgun wound of the chest," and he also suffered multiple wounds of the liver and lungs, and "abrasions of posterior portion of right forearm and right forehead." Temple had received "two shotgun wounds, one in the right breast at the nipple, the other in the lower chest wall on the left side, penetrating his right lung, pancreas, liver, stomach and transverse colon." There was also a "mutilating wound on the back of his left elbow." Although the autopsies did not so indicate, Carl Cooper's family maintained that he was castrated. According to his mother, "He didn't have no front, he didn't have no chest, no stomach, no privates, no organs, or nothing." From the reports of the undertakers, as well as the surviving witnesses, the policemen had mutilated the bodies.

The killings and beatings have been described in great detail by the survivors, and by officers who did not participate in the massacre. One of the three policemen who was later charged with one of the murders said, "We're going to kill all of you black-ass nigger pimps and throw you in the river. We're going to fill up the Detroit River with you pimps and whores." After the first two youths had been murdered, a policeman is reported to have said, "I killed them two motherfuckers." Finally, after the third murder, a policeman remarked to one of the survivors, upon leaving, "We're going to come back and kill all you niggers."

The policemen involved made no report of the deaths to their superiors, and while they claimed initially that their attacks were in response to sniper fire, one report of the incident came to the conclusion "that the killings in the Algiers were not executions of snipers, looters, or arsonists caught red-handed in felonious crimes in the heart of a riot, but rather that they were murders embellished by racist abuse, indiscriminate vengeance, sexual jealousy, voyeurism, wanton blood-letting, and sadistic physical and mental tortures characterized by the tormentors as 'a game.' " In her grief, Aubrey Pollard's mother said, "If those guys [the three policemen] want to fight all that bad, why in the hell don't they go over to Victnam."

After one of the policemen admitted that he killed one of the youths, he was charged with first-degree murder and tried in the summer of 1969. At the same time, the private guard was tried for felonious assault. Both were acquitted, and no charges were brought against the other two policemen. The following January, however, charges of conspiracy to deny the civil rights of the three black youths were brought against the four men. They were tried by an all-white jury in the city of Flint, Michigan, and all were acquitted.

The not guilty verdict was not unexpected; it represented yet another in a long series of cases in which the police have been vindicated for killing black people without provocation. The killings occurred in the midst of the most serious of the recent black uprisings, and when blacks revolt against their oppression—and destroy private property!—it is not surprising that the agents of repression and violence are unleashed in the name of "law and order" to contain them. In such an atmosphere the demoralized police, themselves victims of the same economic exploitation, but motivated by deeply rooted feelings of racism, are unrestrained in their use of force.

The Columbia Bust

Along with blacks and other racial minorities, students have become special targets of police violence. Indeed, in many ways radical college and university students have become "niggers" in the eyes of the police. As one policeman was overheard to have said of students during a Yippie demonstration in New York's Grand Central Station, "If they want to act like niggers, we'll treat them like niggers."

Like the Black Panthers, radical students maintain that most authority in the United States is illegitimate. Consequently, they have challenged the center of this illegitimate authority which is closest to them—their own colleges and universities. In virtually every major college and university in the country, students have demanded an end to racial oppression, an end to American imperialism as manifested in Indochina, and widespread educational reform. To an extent, colleges and universities were attacked by students because they were easy targets. While students can easily seize a college administration building, it is considerably more difficult, if not impossible, to seize the Pentagon, a military installation, a state building, or the headquarters of a large corporation. In addition, however, educational institutions were attacked because while they loudly proclaim political neutrality, they are in fact guilty of racist practices and deeply involved in the support of American imperialism.

Among the most violent confrontations between police and students were those at Columbia University in April and May of 1968. Other violent confrontations have occurred at the University of California at Berkeley and at Santa Barbara, Cornell, Harvard, Howard, Michigan, Wisconsin, Stanford, San Francisco State, Jackson State College in Mississippi, and Kent State University in Ohio, to list only the more highly publicized of these events. But the violence at Columbia was sustained longer than that at any other college or university in the country.

Columbia experienced a number of student demonstrations before the one which paralyzed the university in April 1968. As early as May 1965, a group of students protested the ceremony at which the Naval Officers Training Corps was scheduled to present its annual awards. When the protesting students succeeded in blocking entrance to the ceremony, university administrators summoned police to the campus.

The following year, on November 15, 1966, students protested when a representative of the Central Intelligence Agency visited the campus to interview potential employees. When the CIA suspended the interviews, the protest ended. The following February 18, CIA representatives again appeared on campus but again suspended interviews after students blocked the doors to the rooms in which the interviews were to be held.

In April 1967, a group of some 300 students protested the appearance on campus of recruiters from the United States Marines, and this time the protesters met active opposition from a small group of conservative students. The Marine recruiters suspended their activities for the day but announced that they would resume the following morning. When they returned, the ranks of both groups had increased, with 800 protesting the Marine recruiting and 500 supporting it. While the students were demonstrating, the Marines completed their work and left campus.

Recruiters on the campus from Dow Chemical Company, the manufacturers of napalm, were picketed by some 200 students on February 28, 1968. When the picket line turned into a sit-in, the recruiters canceled appointments they had made. Also in February 1968, many students demonstrated with community residents against the new gymnasium scheduled to be constructed in Morningside Park, a sort of boundary line separating the university from the Harlem community.

Two other demonstrations were held in the spring of 1968 before the massive occupation of university buildings by the students. The first of these was a protest on March 27 against the affiliation of the university with the Institute for Defense Analyses. During this demonstration, students delivered a petition signed by more than 1,500 students and faculty members demanding an end to the university's relationship with the Institute. And at a university-sponsored memorial service for Martin Luther King, Jr., on April 9, a student walked to the speaker's platform and accused the university of "committing an outrage" against the memory of King because of its long record of racism.

With the exception of the 1965 demonstration against the Naval ROTC awards presentation, all the other demonstrations were organized and led by Students for a Democratic Society. Although SDS had the support of other campus organizations, its members were mainly responsible for the events which led to the seizure and occupation of campus buildings, which in turn led to the police bust.

On April 23, SDS planned a demonstration to protest the construction of the gymnasium, the University's affiliation with the Institute for Defense Analyses, and the imposition of discipline on six students without a formal hearing. Some

500 students appeared for the demonstration, including members of the Students Afro-American Society, and then decided to stage a sit-in in Hamilton Hall, a classroom building which also serves as administrative offices for Columbia College. The Dean of the College was held within the building, which the demonstrators then decided to occupy. Later the group agreed that black students would remain in the building and that white students would leave.

The white students left after having been in the building 16 hours and proceeded to occupy Low Library, which houses the offices of the President of the University. Other students occupied Avery Hall, the School of Architecture building; Fayerweather Hall, which houses offices and classrooms for economics, political science and sociology; and Mathematics Hall. It is estimated that some 800 students were in the five buildings when the police were called to remove them. The police were called on Monday afternoon, and by early Tuesday morning the buildings were cleared of students. It is rather widely agreed by observers that the 1,000 members of the New York City Police Department employed widespread violence, often unnecessarily, to accomplish their assigned task.

The most comprehensive account of the violence employed by the police during the Columbia bust is contained in an unofficial report by six graduate students, staff members and attorneys, entitled *Police on Campus*. This report is based on more than 300 eyewitness accounts of the police action at Columbia. It concluded, among other things, that on several occasions the police used unnecessary violence toward students and bystanders; that the police violence at Columbia was not solely a response to provocation; and that the police violence was not an isolated phenomenon limited to a few policemen but that "a very large number of the participating policemen consciously and purposely used excessive force where little or none was required by the circumstances."

The various buildings were cleared by the police in the order in which they were occupied. The black students in Hamilton Hall, in accordance with previously devised plans, offered no resistance. At the other buildings, however, violence was rampant. Faculty members who had stationed themselves at several buildings in order to protest the appearance of the police were indiscriminately beaten. The faculty members wore white armbands to indicate their status, but according to a French instructor: "I was grabbed, spun around, and struck from behind with something hard. According to Professor—— and Professor——, both eyewitnesses who were only a few feet away, one of the attackers withdrew a nightclub from his left sleeve and struck me with it in his right hand. . . . I was knocked to the ground and made to bleed and feel pain. I was admitted to St. Luke's Hospital at 3:00 A.M. where I received four stitches on the back of my head." He continued, ". . . I am certain that the men who attacked us . . . were policemen, as I saw several of them later, inside Low, where I was taken for first aid. They were drinking coffee at the police canteen there." A newspaper reporter at the demonstration saw a plainclothes policeman turn an instructor to the side while another struck him on the head with a club. At about the same time a female teacher was clubbed to the ground by another policeman.

Several persons reported on the police action at Low Library, the first building at which force was used to clear out the students, on the morning of April 30. A graduate student who was inside the building gave this description: "The cops came in swinging their clubs, kicking, and shoving. . . . We tried to hold our positions but did not fight. I was clubbed on the head from behind by what I assumed to be a billy jack. I was about 30 feet from the door by this time and stood up, only to be assailed by another cop who punched me square in the face and sent me flying over the edge onto the lawn by the Foreign Student Center."

A faculty member reports that he was "thrown to the north side of the door by a uniformed policeman and struck in the head by a billy club. I was then struck a second time from behind by another policeman. When I stood up I was hurled back to the ground by a third policeman who struck me two more times in the head."

A 50-year-old medical doctor who was arrested related his experiences at the hands of the police. "I was thrown to the floor, jerked to my feet, choked, clubbed from behind (later requiring five stitches), and dragged bleeding out through the narrow passageway. I suspect that my being the first attacked was to diminish my effectiveness as an observer, but I had time to see students, both men and women, being clubbed freely and dragged in a vicious manner, many by the hair, through the passage. So forceful was the rush that many students were squeezed against the sides of the passageway, and I feared that they would be crushed."

Avery Hall was the third building to be cleared. An inspector instructed the policemen assigned to this building not to use nightsticks, since he did not expect resistance from the building's occupants, and to use restraint. When the police arrived, they found outside the building a contingent of faculty members and students who were opposed to the clearing of the building. The police ignored their instructions. A newspaper reporter described what happened: "The policemen, both uniformed and plainclothesed, punched and kicked the still-seated students. Some policemen repeatedly hit seated students with what appeared to be blackjacks. Other policemen grabbed students from the ground by arms, legs, clothing, hair, anything they could grab. They literally threw students into the air, hurled some over hedges, flung others to the ground several feet away with considerable force."

An undergraduate male student who was seated on the steps of the building gave the following report: "The police could have chosen to carry us off one by one, and they could have done that without any resistance from us. Instead they chose to drag us by the hair and kick us as we 'went limp.' In this manner I was moved approximately thirty feet." He continued, "I found the kicking most objectionable though I received no serious injury. I was not attacking the police, merely refusing to move. . . . Many of the kicks . . . were directed to the area of my groin and anus. One well planted kick managed to swell both the opening of my anus and the area around the urethra at the base of my penis."

The police hastily evacuated Avery Hall, frequently throwing students who were injured on the lawn outside the building. A newspaper reporter present described the scene: "Perhaps a score of students, boys and girls, were bruised, bleeding and crying. Several seemed stunned . . . Robert McG. Thomas, bleeding from scalp lacerations, said he had been beaten by policemen inside the building. . . . A faculty member . . . stood several yards from the Avery entrance with blood streaming down his face from a scalp wound. Asked what happened, he said, 'I was standing in front of the building, I was hit by a policeman.' He appeared to be stunned and said no more." He reports that at least two other persons were stretched out on the grass nearby, apparently unconscious, and that several students used an improvised wooden stretcher to carry the casualties to a nearby first-aid station.

Fayerweather Hall was the next building to be opened and cleared by the police. Unlike Avery Hall, Fayerweather required two hours to be cleared. Upon their arrival the

100 policemen assigned to the building found both entrances blocked by faculty members wearing white arm bands and by students. One faculty member reported his encounter with the police: "I was hit about the shoulders and on the chest and fell back onto the students behind me. I got up and was struck or punched down again. The policemen were frenzied; one shouted at me, 'You fucking pigs.' I was then thrown across a sparse hedge onto the grass beyond. When I looked up I saw that Professor—— was being beaten savagely on the head and shoulders by several policemen, and to his left a student lying on the ground was being kicked by more than one policeman." Finally, he said, a plainclothes policeman "then rushed at me trying to kick me, as I lay on the ground. I rolled and scrambled avoiding his kicks. . . . I got to my feet and ran toward the exit. Someone struck me in the back and I fell again."

A physician who was at Fayerweather to administer first aid described some of the injuries inflicted on the demonstrators: "I administered first aid to as many as forty students suffering from various injuries, mostly lacerations of the scalp and face, and attempted to evacuate as many as possible to a temporary infirmary at Philosophy Hall. Several students I saw complained of having been kicked in the groin and were doubled up with pain. . . . Although most of the injuries I saw cannot be classified as critical, I feel they reflect an undue use of force inappropriate to the nonviolent nature of the student protest."

An undergraduate student, who stood at a barricaded door in Fayerweather Hall, reported that several policemen approached him screaming, "Let's get that little motherfucker first." One policeman struck him in the face with a flashlight. "It struck me slightly over my mouth, opening a gash and numbing my entire face. After that I was rushed by about eight cops who threw me to the floor by my hair and beat me with blackjacks. They surrounded me and kicked me, repeatedly throwing me to the floor as I tried to get up."

Mathematics Hall was the last building to be cleared in the early morning hours of April 30. There, too, the police attacked students, faculty members and bystanders. An undergraduate student reported: "Another student was backing up, facing the police when four police isolated me from the crowd, separating themselves from the wedge and began beating me with riot clubs. I fell down on my knees and they continued beating me on the head and back. My head was opened up and bleeding profusely."

A medical aide who attempted to assist injured students described the scene at Mathematics Hall: "Outside the building these students were dragged along the ground. I saw one boy kicked, and his exposed back scraped along the cement walk. I called to the police to use four men to carry him. They said, 'He can walk if he wants to. He's just getting what he deserves.' I kept walking alongside this youth insisting that they carry him." He reports that behind him he saw two policemen carrying a small female student, twisting her arms. "She cried, 'They're kicking him, make them stop.' I again called to them to stop and continued to follow her to below the steps of Low Library. There the police dropped her. 'Let me take her to a first-aid station. This girl is hurt.' They refused."

A physician reported that a student who indicated his willingness to walk, after having been arrested, was nonetheless beaten: "I walked over to the Mathematics building. They were removing students from the building. I followed this group to the south corner of the Math Building when a student either sat down or slipped. He was surrounded by 10 to 15 policemen. I saw five or six policemen's arms striking at someone on the ground. I heard him say 'I'll walk, I'll walk,' but they continued to strike him. I tried to approach him but the police blocked my access." He identified himself as a doctor and the police threatened to arrest him. "I could get no closer than about six yards. I finally saw him being dragged away, his shirt torn off and semi-conscious."

Because it was fairly well known on campus when the police would be called to clear the buildings, large crowds of people had amassed throughout the campus and the nearby streets to witness the activities. Numerous spectators report having either been beaten by the police or having observed the police beating others. While students are said to have frequently used abusive language, all evidence indicates that the violence was usually initiated by the police. Furthermore, most observers agree that the provocation from the students, faculty members and bystanders was hardly of a nature to justify the extent of force used.

During the first three weeks in May, the police encountered groups of students on and off campus in a variety of violent incidents, such as a mass rally on May 1, called to protest the police action of April 30, and the second occupation of Hamilton Hall on May 21, protesting disciplinary actions against some students. Although conflicting accounts of the number of persons injured during April and May at Columbia have appeared, they all agree that more than 100 were injured to the extent of requiring hospital treatment. According to the university-sponsored report *Crisis at Columbia,* of the persons treated for injuries at nearby hospitals, 14 were policemen. Since several medical clinics had been set up throughout the campus to treat injured students and other university personnel, it is likely that the number of students, faculty members and bystanders injured by the police reached several hundred.

The Mayor of New York City was quoted as saying he believed there was substance to the charges of police brutality at Columbia, and the two comprehensive reports of the events concluded that excessive use of force had characterized the behavior of the police. The actions of New York police at Columbia have since been paralleled by their counterparts at colleges and universities throughout the country.

The occupation of university buildings by students at Columbia University signaled the beginning of a nationwide movement by college and university students to challenge the authority vested in the administrations of these institutions. Colleges and universities have always served the interests of the Establishment, and since World War II they have been deeply involved in the support of American imperialism throughout the world. They have trained hundreds of thousands of military officers; they have developed an enormous arsenal of history's most deadly weapons (including nuclear weapons and poisonous gasses); they have engaged in counter-insurgency research throughout the world to forestall popular liberation movements. In short, they have contributed their faculties and other resources to the maintenance of America's position of economic dominance in the world.

On the domestic scene, the colleges and universities have supported the status quo by the oppression of racial minorities and by training an elite corps of leaders for the corporate power structure. While vigorously proclaiming political neutrality, colleges and universities have steadfastly supported American imperialism at home and abroad, ignoring the wishes and needs of students. When students display compassion for the victims of American imperialism and demand a restructuring of priorities at home and abroad, they threaten the interests of the power structure. These demands for reform, backed by demonstrations and the occupation of buildings, force the agents of the existing order (college and university administrators in this case) to summon police and National Guardsmen to use whatever force is necessary to contain the rebellious students.

In addition to college and university students, however, others throughout the country—usually young people—have also encountered massive police violence. One of the most violent confrontations occurred in Chicago in August 1968.

Police Riot in Chicago

The violence on the part of the police in Chicago in August 1968 was unusual in the extent of its coverage by the mass media and in its scale. Nevertheless, it should not have been surprising. In the spring and summer of 1968, protest demonstrations and marches had occurred throughout the country, frequently resulting in clashes between demonstrators and the police. Whenever such protests occurred, violence on the part of the police was usual. Indeed, one such demonstration in which the police brutalized demonstrators had taken place in Chicago on April 27, at a peace rally. But the demonstrations at the Democratic National Convention were national in scope, and the media coverage was international.

A study team of the National Commission on the Causes and Prevention of Violence issued a report based on more than 3,400 statements of eyewitnesses to the events, 180 hours of motion pictures, and some 12,000 still photographs. This report concluded that ". . . on the part of the police there was enough wild club swinging, enough cries of hatred, enough gratuitous beating to make the conclusion inescapable that individual policemen, and lots of them, committed violent acts far in excess of the requisite force for crowd dispersal or arrest. To read dispassionately the hundreds of statements describing at firsthand the events of Sunday and Monday nights is to become convinced of the presence of what can only be called a police riot."

This report placed the burden for the violence squarely on the Chicago Police Department, whose response to provocations, ranging from obscenities to using such missiles as rocks and sticks, was "unrestrained and indiscriminate" violence. Police violence was not limited to demonstrators, but was inflicted on "onlookers, and large numbers of residents who were simply passing through, or happened to live in the areas where confrontations were occurring." Furthermore, newsmen and news photographers were singled out for assault.

As soon as it was announced in October 1967 that the Democratic Party would hold its national convention in Chicago, dissident groups started planning massive demonstrations to coincide with the convention, at which they assumed Lyndon Johnson would be re-nominated, with Hubert Humphrey again his running mate. When these groups announced plans to demonstrate in Chicago, city officials made elaborate plans to contain the demonstrations. Among the groups who announced their intention to demonstrate were various self-styled revolutionary groups, Communists, civil-rights groups, peace groups, and moderate liberals. Their aim was to protest against the war in Vietnam, racism and other social injustices, and unrepresentative government. Intensive planning and growing disenchantment with American foreign and domestic policies were responsible for the cooperation and involvement of many other groups, including religious groups, peace groups, legal and medical groups, and student groups.

Officials of these groups attempted to negotiate with Chicago city personnel to secure permits for demonstrations, marches and the right to sleep in public parks. At almost every turn they were frustrated by city officials. Determined to exercise their Constitutional rights, demonstration officials continued to make plans, convinced that city officials would ultimately relent. The city of Chicago responded by providing special training to its police force of some 12,000 men, by alerting the Illinois National Guard, and by requesting the assistance of the United States Army.

By the beginning of the convention week, Chicago was an armed camp. Officials of the Democratic Party had turned down suggestions that the convention be moved to a location less likely to generate violence between those whose responsibility it was to maintain public safety and those determined to express their discontent. The advance publicity by the leaders of the demonstrations and by city officials had been so widespread that representatives of news services from around the world converged on the city to report on what seemed destined to be massive clashes between the demonstrators and law enforcement personnel. Indeed, by the time the convention was underway more than 6,000 representatives of the press were in Chicago to cover the events.

The 1968 Democratic National Convention was held from August 26 through August 30. Demonstrators from around the country arrived ahead of the delegates, but while it had been predicted that hundreds of thousands of demonstrators would appear in Chicago, at the peak of the demonstrations it is estimated that the crowd did not exceed 10,000. By August 18 thousands had already arrived, and on August 22 violence flared when a Chicago policeman killed a 17-year-old American Indian who was accused of having fired at him. On August 25 a force of more than 150 policemen charged demonstrators in Lincoln Park who had shouted obscenities at them. It is reported by eye witnesses that the police removed their nameplates and badges, and when demonstrators were knocked down they were beaten. Such violence, which continued throughout the convention week, was documented by a study team of the National Commission on the Causes and Prevention of Violence.

Eyewitnesses reported seeing a 33-year-old school teacher knocked to the ground by the police. When his girl friend attempted to assist him, she was struck repeatedly by six policemen with "batons," as police clubs are delicately called. A criminologist, who was in Chicago to study the convention security procedures, reported that he was struck with a shotgun while attempting to aid a boy who had fallen. The boy was also struck by several policemen. A graduate student was struck on the head with a police baton, and when he raised his hand to his head, two fingers were broken by another blow.

A United States attorney reported that a derelict who appeared to have been drunk asked a policeman a question in response to which the policeman pulled a cannister from his belt and sprayed its contents into the derelict's eyes. The man stumbled and fell on his face. When two girls attempted to assist a youth in the custody of a policeman, they were clubbed on their stomachs, backs and legs by several policemen and finally dragged away and arrested. One demonstrator observed several policemen standing together. One yelled, "Hey, there's a nigger over there we can get," and they then proceeded to beat the middle-aged black man without provocation. A student watching from a hotel window reported having seen two or three policemen grab a young man and beat him until he fell to the ground. Then he was beaten while being dragged to a police van.

A university professor, a member of the committee arranging the demonstrations, was brutally beaten by the police. He suffered severe scalp wounds, body bruises, swollen testes and a multiple fracture of his left hand. He was later arrested and charged with aggravated battery and resisting arrest. A priest reported having seen a boy of 14 or 15 beaten to the ground by the police. When a well-dressed woman, who had also witnessed the beating, complained to a police captain, another policeman sprayed gas in her face and clubbed her to the ground. The two policemen then dragged her to the same police van with the young boy. Finally, a student reported seeing a middle-aged man with tears in his eyes approach a policeman and ask why they were beating people. The policeman responded by striking the man on the head. His glasses fell off, and as he attempted to retrieve them, he was clubbed on the back and head until he could not move.

These are only a few examples of police brutality during the week of the Democratic National Convention. More than 100 civilians were treated for major injuries at Chicago area hospitals, and the Medical Committee for Human Rights compiled its own records of persons treated by its personnel. Altogether, 425 persons were treated at the medical facilities maintained by the Committee; another 200 were treated on the spot by mobile medical teams; another 400 were given first aid for tear gas or Mace. These figures, which are likely to represent an underenumeration, show that more than 1,100 civilians suffered injuries at the hands of the Chicago police during the week. It is probable that many people did not report their injuries, either because they were slight or because they did not want to become involved with authorities.

According to the official records of the police department, a total of 192 policemen reported injuries sustained during the convention week. Of this number, some 49 were hospitalized. Most of the injuries to policemen resulted from flying objects, although some of them reported having been kicked and scratched by demonstrators.

Of the 300 newsmen assigned to cover the demonstrations in the streets and parks during the convention week, more than 65 were injured by the police. The police are said to have believed their treatment of demonstrators was being distorted by the newsmen, and they responded by assaulting newsmen and destroying their equipment. Several newsmen required hospitalization. For example, a news photographer with two cameras and press identification stood on the porch of an apartment house observing a clash between police and demonstrators. Several policemen approached the house, one saying, "Get the man with the camera." When he was ordered by the police to "move on," several of them followed him into the lobby as he attempted to obey, and one of them clubbed him on the head. They ignored his plea for an ambulance, and he was later driven to a hospital by a friend.

A reporter wearing his convention credentials observed the police beating a girl and stopped to take notes. Saying, "Give me that god damn notebook, you dirty bastard," another policeman stepped forward, threw the notebook in the gutter, and clubbed the reporter several times on the head. A fellow reporter took him to a hospital, where he was treated for a contusion and abrasions of the scalp. The following day he was admitted to the hospital, where he remained for 36 hours.

A television cameraman filming a demonstration was approached from behind by 10 or 12 policemen, one of whom hit him on the head with his club, opening a scalp wound that required seven stitches at a local hospital. At the time of the attack the cameraman was wearing his press credentials, and his camera was labeled on both sides with the call letters of the television network.

At Lincoln Park, a reporter for a Chicago newspaper was observing the melee when three policemen approached and ordered him to leave. The reporter pointed out that he was from the press and presented his credentials. He was struck from behind, fell to the ground, and was clubbed several times on the back. He suffered bruises and temporary paralysis of the left side.

Among the newsmen injured were representatives of a French news magazine and a British newspaper. In ten cases, photographic and recording equipment were deliberately smashed by the police. Inside the amphitheatre, while the convention was in progress, a reporter from a major television network was attacked in full view of millions of viewers by a plainclothesman later identified as a security guard for the convention. Most of the newspapers, the American Newspaper Guild and the radio and television networks protested about the police brutality inflicted on their employees. In response to mounting criticism, Mayor Daley of Chicago called a press conference and charged that the efforts of law enforcement personnel were being "twisted and distorted" in the news accounts.

The behavior of the Chicago police during the Democratic National Convention received widespread coverage throughout the world. Because so many people either watched the events on television or read the news accounts, usually accompanied by photographs, it was impossible to conceal what had happened. For nearly a week Chicago was the scene of one of the most violent civilian-police confrontations in modern history. And while the police were frequently provoked by the demonstrators, their response was grossly out of proportion to the provocation.

Contrary to the interpretation of the study team of the National Commission on the Causes and Prevention of Violence, the police violence in Chicago was not caused merely by acts of excessive force by "individual policemen"; nor was it only a response on the part of the Chicago Police Department to minor provocations by demonstrators. While the police indeed brutalized thousands of citizens, it was not simply that the police themselves misbehaved. They acted as the agents of a social order fearful of any challenge to its status. And police, of course, are given immunity from prosecution for the use of whatever force is necessary to maintain the status quo. In Chicago, American law was once again turned against the people it is ostensibly designed to protect.

In a period of widespread social protest, the police find themselves at odds with increasing numbers of protesters, especially blacks, students, and others who protest against the war. And since the vast majority of citizens share the conservative views of the police on these issues, the brutality of police is condoned and reinforced. In the decade of the 1960's, however, police violence against blacks, students and other anti-war protesters went far beyond even the extensive violence of the larger American society.

Members of the New Left refer to the police as "pigs," meaning, according to the Black Panther Party which is responsible for this label, that the police are "ill-natured beasts who have no respect for law and order," and that they are "foul traducers who usually masquerade as victims of unprovoked attacks." Whatever one might think of this designation or its originators, who themselves admit that "there are a few good policemen," support for this characterization of American policemen is not lacking. Observers from the President's Commission on Crime and Law Enforcement found that some policemen on occasion carry knives in order to plant them on anyone they might kill and be able to claim that the shooting was done in self-defense.

Furthermore, in his comparative study of police practices in Western European countries and the United States, George Berkley found that especially in regard to reliance on the use of force and in the practice of corruption, American policemen more closely resemble those of Hitler's Germany and Mussolini's Italy than those of England, France, Sweden and West Germany. In a society where violence is so extensive, it is not surprising that the police have come to rely on force in dealing with citizens; and because they are generally responsible only to other policemen, American police are able to commit the most serious crimes against innocent citizens, claiming self-defense, and be assured of vindication. The search-and-destroy missions against members of the Black Panther Party serve to illustrate this technique.

In the European countries studied by Berkley, the police pride themselves on the use of minimal force against citizens. When they carry handguns, as most of them do, the guns are of light caliber, and their clubs are made of rubber so that if used they do not break bones or leave scars. In the United States, on the other hand, all policemen are armed with powerful weapons and their clubs are made of hard wood. In Memphis, Tennessee, for example, the *New York Times* reported that police shot and killed eight persons in the first five months of 1970. In that department the police used what are called "nonricocheting hollow bullets," a variation of the dumdum bullet which expands when it hits its target. Although these bullets have been outlawed in warfare since the Hague Convention of 1907, which the United

States signed, the chief of police in Memphis insists that they are used for safety reasons, that is, to reduce danger to innocent bystanders.

American policemen are six times more likely to kill than be killed, while in the European countries studied by Berkley far more policemen are killed by civilians than kill civilians. In Sweden, for example, over a two and one-half year period, four policemen were killed by citizens, while during that period *and* the preceeding seven years, only two citizens were killed by policemen. In France, 18 policemen were killed in the line of duty in 1965, while police were responsible for five deaths. And in England the police virtually never kill people, since they do not carry lethal weapons, although they themselves are sometimes killed by criminals. Furthermore, after three policemen were shot and killed in a single incident in London in 1966, there were demands from citizens that the police be armed with lethal weapons for use in self-defense. But the Police Federation was so strongly opposed to this idea that many of its members threatened to resign if the decision was made to arm them. The following year the police in England even rejected a proposal that they be armed with such nonlethal weapons as chemical sprays.

The police in the United States insist upon being heavily armed, and they are usually rewarded for so-called heroic acts in armed confrontations with citizens, frequently earning medals or promotions for such acts. In some sections of the country they not only encourage the ownership of weapons by citizens but set up classes to teach them how to use these weapons. Moreover, the killing of black youths by police is so widespread that the National Council of Police Societies, an organization of black law officers, expressed concern about the practice at its 1970 annual meeting and offered resolutions aimed at curbing it. One resolution read:

"We urge that police departments rapidly acquire nonlethal weapons such as the tranquilizing instruments developed at the Carnegie-Mellon University in Pittsburgh. Such weapons are now used by animal handlers in national parks and in zoos, indicating that the nation considers animals more important than some human beings."

Hundreds of black youths are killed each year, and thousands more are injured by trigger-happy policemen. For example, according to the *New York Times,* 46 black youths were shot in a disturbance in Asbury Park, New Jersey, on July 7, 1970. The police claimed they had only fired their weapons into the air to warn the demonstrators, and when asked how there could be so many cases of gunshot wounds, a police sergeant who served as spokesman replied: "That's all the information I have."

Police work is difficult in a society which has permitted social problems to spread and intensify, as is the situation in the United States. But the police have insisted upon seeing virtually all poor and non-conforming citizens as their enemies. Nevertheless, citizens in slum sections of cities demand greater police presence even though they realize that the police regard them as the enemy and even though they reciprocate in their feelings about the police. If the police were capable of responding to all citizens as human beings, the antipathy which is so often displayed toward them would no doubt become transformed into feelings of respect. But so long as they maintain the position that "respect for the police in tough neighborhoods depends on the willingness of patrolmen to use force, frequently and effectively," as a majority of the police in New York City asserted in a survey, the police will continue to be among the most feared and hated categories of citizens in the country.

Most studies of police maintain that on personality characteristics such as authoritarianism and prejudice, they do not differ from American citizens in general. They maintain that no special personality characteristics predispose individuals to engage in an occupation in which force against others is often required. Yet many studies and newspaper accounts have detailed the extent of right-wing sentiment in police departments throughout the country. Police are often members of the John Birch Society, the Ku Klux Klan, the Minutemen and other right-wing groups. Furthermore, they frequently support the most conservative candidates for political office, such as George Wallace of Alabama and Barry Goldwater of Arizona.

Newspaper accounts have recently indicated that friction between black and white policemen is extensive. A near race riot occurred during the annual policemen's picnic in Pittsburgh in the summer of 1970. According to a black police official, the incident stemmed from resentment generated among white policemen when a black policeman danced with a white woman. And in many other cities around the country, tensions mount as black policemen organize themselves and protest brutality against other blacks by white policemen. According to John Darnton, writing in the *New York Times,* these tensions have virtually polarized most large city police departments into two hostile camps. He attributes these developments to increasing numbers of young black policemen, often from the slums; to the large number of new organizations of black policemen; to discrimination against blacks in police departments; to the prevalence of right-wing, anti-black conservatism among white policemen; and to such events as the black uprisings and the call for "law and order" by political candidates.

Just as nearly all black citizens have either experienced police brutality directly or know someone who has, virtually every black policeman has witnessed acts of brutality by white policemen against black people, and a series of black-white confrontations within police departments has resulted from such acts. While the brutalization of blacks might have gone unnoticed by black policemen a few years ago, the younger black policeman is no longer willing to permit such behavior without protest. As a young black police officer in Chicago remarked, "We're black men first, and then we're police officers." And the Officers for Justice in San Francisco have adopted a pledge which reads in part: "We will no longer permit ourselves to be relegated to the role of brutal pawns in a chess game affecting the communities in which we serve. We are husbands, fathers, brothers, neighbors and members of the black community. Donning the blue uniform has not changed this."

One of the primary functions of the police is to maintain the status quo. They are the agents of a social-political-economic order which uses them for its protection. When Black Panthers arm themselves and advocate the abolition of capitalism, they are threats to this order. When black people in cities destroy private property, they too are threats. When college and university students seize buildings and demand an end to domestic and foreign imperialism, students too are threats. And when thousands of citizens challenge the legitimacy of authority by demonstrating in the streets, the threat is intensified. The response of a threatened establishment is to unleash the forces of repression and violence always at its command, including the police. It is unlikely, therefore, that any significant reform in police practices will be effected in this country before the United States itself is transformed into a more humane society.

V I

►►►►►►

Cultural Supports for Violence

That the United States continues to be one of the most violent of societies seems well established, although little recognition of this cultural trait was acknowledged prior to the decade of the 1960's. Since the late 1960's, however, a series of books have appeared on the subject of violence in the United States. These books represent a growing recognition that not only is the American Government the "greatest purveyor of violence in the world today," as the late Martin Luther King, Jr., himself a victim of America's violence, asserted in 1967, but that widespread violence has been an integral part of American life from the beginning. The National Commission on the Causes and Prevention of Violence, recognizing this tradition of violence in the country, has asserted that "America has always been a relatively violent nation. Considering the tumultuous historical forces that have shaped the United States, it would be astonishing were it otherwise." It concluded this section of its final report by noting that "Violence has usually been the lava flowing from the top of the volcano fed by deeper fires of social dislocation and injustice."

The available evidence destroys the long-standing myth of nonviolence in the United States, and supports the contention that a more accurate characterization of the country is that it indeed represents a culture of violence. In addition to its bloody history and the tradition of violence which it established, America continues to be a violent society because the social climate is conducive to such behavior; that is, violent behavior is encouraged, rewarded and facilitated by cultural factors. Throughout its history the use of force has been valued by Americans as an effective means of dealing with a variety of problems, especially the resolution of conflict. Such behavior has become institutionalized, and while certain forms of violence are not openly encouraged, others such as war and capital punishment have received official sanction in the society.

Violence in America appears to have accelerated with increasing urbanization. For example, although its data are inadequate and questionable, the Federal Bureau of Investigation maintains that the crime rate, including crimes of violence, increased by 148 percent between 1960 and 1969. But as is typical, public officials respond to increasing violence by more punitive measures rather than by attempting to alleviate the causes of such behavior. Convinced that the society is a humane and just one, they are unwilling to consider basic changes in its structure. Several investigatory commissions have recently made recommendations aimed at curbing violence in the society, but these are usually ignored or met with contempt in official circles. And in characteristic American fashion, social problems are permitted to grow until they reach crisis proportions. It is the opinion of the members of the National Commission on the Causes and Prevention of Violence that such a crisis exists in the United States because of the prevalence of violence at the present time. In its final report the Commission warned that "The greatness and durability of most civilizations has been finally determined by how they have responded to . . . challenges from within. Ours will be no exception."

Much of the violence which persists in the United States is a result of the society's having broken faith with the people. Citizens have always expected to be able to live decent lives free from constant frustration and anxiety, as they have been promised by their leaders. After World War II Americans expected to live their lives free from the fear of another war but were caught up immediately in the tensions of the Cold War. While the Cold War generated vast profits for some and made for economic prosperity for most of the nation, it was accompanied by a period of frustration and fear. Most citizens supported the anti-Communism of the Cold War because they were gullible enough to believe their leaders when they condemned Communism simply as a system which was Godless and evil, rather than one which was a threat to the profit system because it was an economic competitor. Nevertheless, in their general state of frustration over war and every other anxiety of their lives, citizens are willing to strike out against any person or group they see as a threat: blacks, long-haired youths, homosexuals and others who deviate from the norms of the society, even their families, friends or anyone who happens to be a convenient target for the release of their frustrations. And a number of cultural elements encourage and nourish this recourse to violence.

Anti-Humanitarian Ethos

Perhaps the single most important contributor to the widespread violence which has plagued the United States from its very beginnings as a nation is the anti-humanitarian ethos which pervades the society. Such a national attitude is manifested in a variety of forms, ranging from the relationship of individual citizens toward each other to the relationship of government officials toward citizens and in relations with other countries. While Americans think of themselves and their government as being basically humanitarian, a cursory examination of widely shared values and practices at all levels of the society reveals that this is something akin to an act of national self-deception. It would be difficult for citizens on a wide scale to be committed to values which indicate a high regard for human beings, while at the same time their government sanctions acts of violence almost without parallel in human history. In Southeast Asia servicemen are rewarded for acts of brutality, including the burning of Vietnamese women and children with napalm, yet Americans naively express shock when comparable acts take place at home. When American servicemen who massacre innocent Vietnamese women and children are congratulated by the American commander of all forces in South Vietnam for dealing the "enemy" a "heavy blow," Americans at home condemn not those who commit the atrocities, those who order them, or the government's policy which makes them possible, but those with enough humanity left to reveal them.

In the spring of 1970, when the President of the United States ordered the extension of the war from Vietnam into Cambodia, hundreds of thousands of college students decided to protest. The President responded to their expressions of dissent by referring to them as "bums," and as these protests escalated, four innocent students were killed by trigger-happy National Guardsmen at Kent State University of Ohio. The following day the President issued, through an intermediary, a cynical and heartless statement in which he said that the tragedy "should remind us all once again that when dissent turns to violence, it invites tragedy." He transfered the blame for the killings from those who were responsible to the victims, an age-old American method of deception.

The anti-humanitarian ethos of American society is probably best illustrated on the national level by the distorted priorities of the country. In his budget message to Congress for Fiscal Year 1971, the President announced that "For the first time in two full decades, the Federal Government will spend more money on human resource programs than on national defense." He estimated budget outlays for the fiscal year at $200.8 billion. Of this money some $73.6 billion, or 37 percent of the total, was allocated for what is called "national defense," the largest single item in the budget. This represents a decline from 50 percent in 1960, but is still considerably more than the national budgets of most of the countries in the world. At the time of the message, for example, a total of more than $180 billion had already been spent in destroying the people of Indochina and their culture.

Another $3.4 billion in the budget was allocated for "space research and technology," and a total of some $8.8 billion was allocated for "commerce and transportation." These figures are in contrast to a total of $26.9 billion for the three crucial programs of education and manpower, health, and community development and housing. This means that nearly three times as much was allocated for military and space spending as was allocated for community development, education and health.

In his message the President promised to "enhance the quality of life" for Americans, yet he later vetoed a substantial Health, Education and Welfare bill on the grounds that it was inflationary. And shortly thereafter he allocated an additional $50 million for the so-called Safeguard missile program, which a great many competent authorities agree is both unnecessary and unworkable. The quality of life in America is not likely to be improved by such priorities as those reflected in the national budget. Thousands of citizens suffer each year from malnutrition. Millions are forced to live in unsafe and substandard housing. Public schools are so inadequately financed and overcrowded that a great deal of what passes for education is little more than a farce. Federal appropriations for medical care and research have been so drastically cut that some medical schools and hospitals are on the verge of closing. The physical environment in which citizens are forced to live is becoming a major menace—the air is polluted, rivers and lakes are contaminated, and the earth's surface has been defiled.

The money spent to destroy a peasant people in Asia could have gone a long way toward alleviating many of the country's domestic problems. Furthermore, between 1946 and 1969, the Government of the United States spent $1,000 billion on what is called defense, often a euphemism for aggressive warfare. The wealth which this figure represents, if properly used, could have gone a long way toward alleviating hunger in the world, creating the technology for increasing food production, and cleaning up the earth's atmosphere. But not only are the leaders of the country indifferent to the plight of people elsewhere in the world, they are willing to permit millions of their own citizens to go hungry, and countless additional millions to live lives of utter degradation. It is nothing short of a crime against humanity that six percent of the world's population should callously exploit half of the world's resources, and use the wealth derived from them to benefit a few, while at the same time destroying millions of the earth's people.

If public resource programs threaten the profits of large corporations, they are not carried out. Private builders do not want money spent for public housing, which would reduce their market. If the Government allocated funds for adequate public transportation systems in and between cities, the automobile industry would lose business. The Federal Government spends enormous sums for highway construction, thereby encouraging citizens to purchase automobiles. The same holds for health care: if the Government provided sufficient tax money for public hospitals, the profits of private entrepreneurs would be threatened.

What businessmen want the Government to do is spend money where it does not compete with private profits. Public money is spent for projects such as the recent $30-plus billions spent to collect rocks on the moon, a dubious antiballistic missiles program, and the development of a supersonic air transport plane to enable the affluent to reduce flying time to Europe by two-thirds. The money is almost literally thrown away rather than used for the immediate needs of citizens.

The persistence of poverty in the United States at a time when a President can publicly boast that "Our nation's industries, shops and farms prosper . . . far beyond the dreams of any people, any time, anywhere," is a serious indictment of a system which has the potential for creating a society worthy of human beings, and of a people who permit this distortion of priorities to develop and persist. The notion of social justice has never been widely shared in the United States. The general feeling is that while citizens have responsibilities toward their government, the government has few, if any, toward citizens. The individual is left to fend for himself in a system which rewards the accumulation of wealth, regardless of how it is done.

Nearly half (more than 45 percent) of the fiscal 1970 federal budget receipts, some $91 billion, is derived from individual income taxes. Overall, the Federal Government collects about two-thirds of all tax receipts. Yet a major share of the responsibility for financing such citizen-oriented programs as housing, medical care, education, public transportation and other community services is left to states and cities, political subdivisions which are clearly unable to finance these programs. Consequently, needy citizens are forced to live in cities which are becoming increasingly uninhabitable, except for the rich. The Federal Government has elected virtually to ignore the urban poor except in drafting them to fight wars of aggression, in matters of taxation, and in confronting them with its uniformed troops during black uprisings.

In 1968 poor Americans, under the sponsorship of the Southern Christian Leadership Conference, organized the Poor People's Campaign to demand an end to poverty and racism in the United States. One of the main events of the campaign was the erection of a shantytown on the Mall at the Lincoln Memorial in Washington to house thousands of blacks, American Indians, Mexican-Americans, Puerto Ricans and poor whites. Operating on the premise that poverty, illiteracy, disease and destitution are unnecessary in the United States at the present time, these citizens journeyed from all parts of the country to petition their government for redress of obvious and legitimate grievances. They were permitted to camp out on the mall for several weeks, but then government officials ordered their shantytown bulldozed. Within a few weeks its residents, who had vowed to remain in Washington until corrective action came from the government, were back in their shanties in their native states. The Poor People's Campaign was ignored by a federal government more concerned with destroying peasants in Asia than with alleviating human misery at home. The organizers of the Campaign did not understand the nature of the American system; given its overriding concern with private profits, the response of the Government should not have been unexpected.

One local incident which clearly illustrates the anti-humanitarian, ruthless character of the society occurred in Berkeley, California, in the spring of 1969. Several non-conformist local residents, called "street people," decided that since a lot owned by the University of California was unused, "something nice" for all the people in the area should be created there. A meeting was held and those in attendance decided to create a public park, a people's park, on the site. Local residents ("straight people"), street people, children, and students from the university cooperated in raising money for the People's Park. The idea was supported by local newspapers, and funds and supplies were solicited from local garden supply stores and other merchants and residents. On Sunday, April 20, some 100 people moved onto the lot, armed with supplies and materials for transforming it into a park, and by May 11 the People's Park was officially dedicated by local ministers.

Officials of the University became apprehensive about the People's Park and attempted to assert the University's ownership by erecting a fence and excluding unauthorized persons from entering the lot. In the early morning hours of May 16, about 70 street people who were either sitting or sleeping in the park were forced to leave as some 200 to 250 policemen from Berkeley, Alameda County and the university invaded the area, equipped with rifles, shotguns and tear gas, and evicted all persons from the park. At six o'clock a construction crew arrived and by mid-afternoon an eight-foot fence had been erected around the People's Park.

A protest rally was convened on campus at noon, attracting some 3,000 people. The crowd marched to the park, which was surrounded by policemen, and threw rocks and bottles at the police. The police responded by releasing tear gas and adding reinforcements, bringing their number to about 600. A rock was alleged to have been thrown from the roof of an adjacent building, and the police fired without warning into the crowd standing on the roof. That was the beginning of a confrontation during which one man was killed by the police, another blinded, some 200 injured, and 920 arrested.

The following day some 2,200 National Guardsmen appeared with rifles, bayonets and tear gas to join the law enforcement personnel. The city of Berkeley was occupied. On Tuesday, May 20, the demonstrators, numbering some 3,000, started a peaceful march through the city of Berkeley. They were stopped by the police, and then assembled for a rally on campus. During the rally a National Guard helicopter flew over the center of the campus and spewed CS gas (which is outlawed by the Geneva Conventions) on the demonstrators, bystanders, university employees, and patients in a hospital. Gas was also thrown into a student snack bar, a classroom and an office.

Officials of the University of California succeeded in destroying the People's Park and in demonstrating the pervasiveness of the anti-humanitarian ethos of the larger society. The land on which the People's Park was created was unused, but rather than permit people to create something of beauty and utility to be used by all, the university unleashed the forces of repression. The People's Park was a threat to the existing order because the people expropriated private property, an act not unlike the seizure of American businesses in Latin American countries. If the people had been permitted to take this land, other groups might have attempted similar seizures elsewhere. This would be a declaration of war against private property, the cornerstone of capitalism.

Public opinion polls show that most Americans support capital punishment. In international relations, most of them supported the continued bombing of North Vietnam. A significant proportion of them advocated the use of nuclear weapons to achieve a military victory in Vietnam. In the eyes of most ordinary citizens, apparently, murder is legitimate so long as it is accomplished by the state, and the killing of those defined by the Department of State as the "enemy" is somehow qualitatively different from homicide. In interpersonal relations, American citizens, like their government, display little regard for their fellow men. Welfare recipients often spy on their neighbors. Dozens of citizens are willing to watch while a defenseless woman is murdered. And in Albany, New York, a large crowd of spectators shouted encouragement to a man threatening to commit suicide, and when he failed to jump from the roof of a building they roared their disappointment.

The citizens of this country, like their leaders, have little regard for human life and human dignity. They may never have engaged in overt acts of violence against other human beings; yet they support such acts, or at the very least are content to tolerate them without dissent. Through the centuries Americans have lived in a society which has demonstrated its contempt for human beings in countless ways. Given the nature of the society, with its emphasis on creating profits rather than serving human needs, it is not surprising that Americans are a violent people. They are turned into brutes by a society devoid of humanism, and the mass media makes its contribution by glorifying brutality.

The Mass Media

The influence of the mass media in generating violent behavior in citizens continues to be a subject of controversy in the United States, but there is growing evidence in support of a direct relationship between violence portrayed on television and in the movies, and subsequent aggressive acts by viewers. Three different schools of thought about this relationship exist. One maintains that violence in the media stimulates violence in real life; another holds that the portrayal of violence drains off aggressive tendencies in viewers and readers; the third school holds that any relationship between violence in the media and violence in real life is not proved.

Television, the youngest of the media, is probably the most influential. Americans spend more time viewing television than they do viewing movies, or reading. Virtually all (at least 95 percent) American homes have at least one television set, and it is estimated that the average set is in use about 40 hours each week. Television has an especially strong appeal for children, and the younger ones are uncritical in the selection of programs. The National Commission on the Causes and Prevention of Violence estimates that children and adolescents spend at least as much time before the television set as they do in school.

Television presents its viewers a steady dose of violence, both in its dramatic programs and in its news presentations. For example, the media task force of the National Commission on the Causes and Prevention of Violence studied the programming of the three major television networks and found that eight out of every 10 dramatic programs in 1967 and 1968 contained some violence. Virtually all of the crime, western, and action-adventure programs (comprising about two-thirds of all the dramatic programs) contained violence, averaging approximately nine episodes of violence each hour. Probably most damaging of all, almost all of the children's cartoon programs on Saturday mornings contained violence, at a rate of more than 20 episodes each hour.

A university research team surveyed the television programming for one week in a major city and in a five-day period recorded the following: one stabbing in the back, four suicide attempts, four persons pushed over cliffs, two cars rolling off cliffs, two attempts to run cars over persons on the sidewalk, a psychotic loose on an airliner, two mob scenes, a horse grinding a man under his hooves, 12 murders, 16 gunfights, 37 hand-to-hand fights, one attempted murder with a pitchfork, two stranglings, and many more episodes of violence.

In television programming, individuals who commit acts of violence are most often portrayed as acting in their own self-interest, and frequently their acts are seen as successful means of attaining the desired end. While it is true that many of the violent episodes presented attempt to convey the impression that violent behavior is not rewarded, the consequences of engaging in such behavior as presented to viewers are often minimal. Furthermore, violence presented in children's programs is rarely seen as painful; it is for the most part glamorized.

Young children are frequently unable to distinguish between fantasy and reality, and there is evidence that the presentation of violence to children on television often reduces their inhibitions against such behavior. After reviewing the evidence, the National Commission on the Causes and Prevention of Violence concluded that ". . . a constant diet of violent behavior on television has an adverse effect on human character and attitudes. Violence on television encourages violent forms of behavior, and fosters moral and social values about violence in daily life which are unacceptable in civilized society." Furthermore, the Commission's media task force found only one study presenting evidence for the theory that TV violence provides a healthy release of hostility in the viewer. While the portrayal of violence in television programming is certainly not the major factor in such behavior among the young, for the society was a violent one before the advent of this medium, it is increasingly clear that television is responsible for generating a share of our national violent behavior.

Television network officials, citing program ratings, justify their programming by insisting that they are merely giving the public programs which it wants to view. And to a great extent this is no doubt true. However, since television uses public airways for its broadcasting, it has an obligation to the public which is greater than catering to its most base desires. Television has an educational function, or should have, to which it is supposedly bound by the regulations under which it operates.

The film industry, like television, is concerned with generating profits. Throughout its history the subject of violence has had a central place in movies, and although the most recent updating of the code of self-regulation stipulates that "Detailed and protracted acts of brutality, cruelty, physical violence, torture and abuse shall not be presented," the code is so often violated as to be nonexistent. Movies depicting violence attract large audiences, and in recent years there has been an increase in their number.

The recent increase in violence in films is apparently an

attempt on the part of the moviemakers to please what they judge to be an increasingly violent movie-going public, and if financial returns are any indication of success, they are correct in their judgment. If movies are to accurately depict many aspects of American life, of course, murder and various forms of brutality cannot be avoided. Moreover, while individuals exposed to acts of violence in movies as well as television are more likely than those not so exposed to engage in subsequent violent behavior, movies are likely to exert less influence in this regard because the audience can be regulated. In most cases children are denied entrance to movies in which violence is portrayed on a wide scale.

The mass media make their contribution to the culture of violence in the United States by presenting constant examples of acts of violence and vividly describing acts of cruelty. After such experiences, already angry and violence-prone citizens can easily purchase firearms to put into practice what they have viewed.

Prevalence of Firearms

In the United States firearms are inexpensive and widely owned. The National Rifle Association, which operates one of the most powerful lobbies against stringent gun control laws, has urged gun lovers to arm themselves with shotguns, ax handles and sledges to protect their neighborhoods against urban rioters (i.e., blacks) as a means of "stabilizing" their communities. Judging from increased purchases of firearms in recent years, their advice has been taken seriously by millions of Americans.

The Second Amendment to the Constitution of the United States is frequently interpreted to mean that citizens have the right to keep and bear arms. This amendment reads: "A well regulated militia being necessary to the security of a free State, the right of the people to keep and bear arms shall not be infringed." But to interpret this amendment as giving individual citizens of contemporary America the right to freely possess dangerous firearms is to distort both its meaning and intent.

The first federal firearms control law, enacted in 1934, applied to machine guns, rifles and shotguns, but not to handguns. Since that time other federal laws have been passed to control the possession of firearms, including the Gun Control Act of 1968, which followed the assassinations of Martin Luther King, Jr. and Robert F. Kennedy, and which pertains mainly to the interstate flow of guns. However, no federal law has yet been enacted which effectively reduces the possession of firearms in the United States. Nor has an elaborate network of some 2,000 state and local laws succeeded in curbing the possession of firearms.

The result is that Americans, more than any other people in the world, are able to own destructive weapons for private use. It is reported that there are some 90 million firearms in civilian hands in the United States, stored in one-half of the 60 million American households, which means that many families have more than one firearm. Most countries in the world, however, especially industrialized nations, have enacted strict laws regarding the possession of firearms, and some countries prohibit the private ownership of most types of firearms. Consequently, firearms are far less widely owned in most countries than in the United States. For example, in the United States there are 13,500 handguns for every 100,000 citizens, compared with fewer than 500 for the same population of Finland, Great Britain, Greece, Ireland and the Netherlands. Austria and Canada have a rate of ownership of 3,000 handguns for every 100,000 citizens.

Furthermore, Americans are purchasing guns at a higher rate than ever before. The National Commission on the Causes and Prevention of Violence reports that between 1962 and 1968 sales of long guns doubled and sales of handguns quadrupled. It is unlikely that the increased sale of handguns resulted from a suddenly increased interest in sports. The grim fact is that these arms are being stored for use against fellow citizens.

Is there any connection between the widespread possession of firearms and the prevalence of violence in America? While the two phenomena are associated, it is impossible to posit a causal relationship between them. However, data provided by the National Commission on the Causes and Prevention of Violence clearly establish a relationship between firearms and three crimes of violence—homicide, aggravated assault and armed robbery. Two-thirds of all homicides, nearly two-fifths of all robberies, and one-fifth of all aggravated assaults are committed with the use of firearms, usually handguns. Furthermore, attacks with firearms are more likely to result in death or serious injury than attacks with any other weapons. Just as the extent of the possession of firearms has increased in recent years, so has the number of homicides in which firearms were used. In the last half of the 1960's, the number of homicides in which firearms were used increased by 50 percent. And throughout the country those areas with the highest concentration of firearms are precisely those with the highest incidence of violent crime.

The prevalence of ownership of firearms by civilians in the United States indicates a loss of faith in the society by its citizens. Citizens in the jungle of American cities purchase firearms as a means of protecting themselves and their property because society has failed to provide this protection.

People in the cities are terrified, and the crime statistics in any urban area fully justify their fears.

While the availability of firearms is only one contributing factor to the prevalence of violence in the United States, it is nevertheless an important one. If the person intent on killing another did not own a handgun, he would perhaps resort to other means, depending upon the seriousness of his intent, but other weapons are less likely to inflict fatal injuries. Since firearms, the most deadly of weapons, are easy to acquire, killing itself is also easy.

In the black community, the control of firearms poses even more serious problems than in the society at large. Although it is true that most homicides and acts of aggravated assault are committed by relatives of the victims or by persons who are acquainted with the victims, many people in the black community feel, and not without justification, that so long as the police are heavily armed and exercise little restraint in the use of firearms where blacks are concerned, they must arm themselves in self-defense. Any effective control of guns in the black community is therefore dependent upon a cessation of the widespread killing of black people by the police. In fact, such killings appear to have accelerated with increasing black militance, and since activities associated with this phenomenon are not likely to diminish in the near future, violence between blacks and the police is more likely to increase than decline. In the meantime, a small percentage of the firearms in the society is in the possession of blacks.

In addition to the ease with which firearms are acquired by civilians, other factors contribute to the high level of violence in America. Another such factor is America's climate of anti-Communism.

Anti-Communism

The climate of anti-Communism in the United States is such that violence committed in what are considered to be acts of patriotism is either rewarded or ignored by law enforcement personnel. Most Americans have been deluded into a hysterical fear of Communism by a ruling class which is threatened by competition from a rival power and an alternative economic system. Since it has been accepted that the spread of Communism must be resisted at all costs, anyone at home or abroad who opposes America's vested economic interests can be labeled a Communist, and violence against such persons is not only sanctioned but rewarded.

The fear of Communism has been used as a pretext to spend money on armaments which have generated vast profits and to divert the attention and energies of working people from the real source of their frustrations at home. For frustrated and fearful Americans, to attack opponents of their country's policies is especially rewarding. Two recent examples from New York City serve to illustrate the point.

In May 1967, supporters of America's policies in Vietnam, angered by a massive rally of citizens dissenting from these policies the month before, staged a parade to "Support Our Boys in Vietnam" on New York's Fifth Avenue. The parade was made up of members of the American Legion, Veterans of Foreign Wars, the International Longshoremen's Association, the Teamsters Union, the John Birch Society, the Conservative Party, a group of priests and nuns, Cuban exiles, and various other groups of individuals. They carried a variety of banners and placards, with such messages as "Kill a Commie for Christ," "Bomb Hanoi," "Draft Martin Luther King," and others.

As it turned out, the participants in the parade not only carried signs advocating violence; they brutalized several innocent people. A black woman, for example, stood silently on the sideline with a sign reading, "No Vietnamese Ever Called Me Nigger." Marchers shouted at her, and one man who was wearing an American Legion uniform left the line, took the sign from her and punched her in the face. About 20 other marchers broke from the line, punched and kicked the fallen woman. Finally six policemen rescued her, but no arrests were made.

Members of the Teamsters Union beat, tarred and feathered a teenager simply because he was wearing sandals and long hair. Again no arrests were made, and on a televised news program his attackers admitted that they were responsible for the act. One lamented that he reached the scene too late "to get in a good punch or kick." When questioned about their actions by a reporter, another replied: "I would like to have left him dead."

At one of the staging points for the parade, residents of a third-floor apartment on Madison Avenue hung a sign, hand-painted on a sheet, from the window of their living room. The sign read, "End the War in Vietnam Now." A group of American Legionnaires saw the sign and responded by throwing rocks and empty beer cans into the window, breaking furniture. The occupants were held hostage in the apartment for hours, and when news of the incident appeared in the newspapers, along with their names and address, they were deluged with hate mail. Although the incident was televised, no attempt was made to apprehend the vandals.

Later in the afternoon, a group of young boys and girls

carrying daisies and dandelions and American flags, who called themselves the Flower Brigade, requested permission to join the parade because they supported American troops but were opposed to the country's foreign policy. Permission was granted by parade officials for them to march, although some of the other marchers objected to the presence of "hippies," and the Boy Scouts, who were marching next to them, moved away. Suddenly, the youngsters were attacked by the marchers, who shouted "Kill them" and "Murder the bastards." The flags were ripped from their hands, and they were beaten by men old enough to be their fathers and grandfathers. As they were being beaten, women cheered (like their counterparts at lynchings in the South). Finally, red paint was thrown in the children's faces and hair, and it was ultimately necessary for police to fight through the mob to rescue them. Again, no arrests were made.

The long-haired teenager, the people in the Madison Avenue apartment who peacefully expressed their opposition to the war, and the children in the Flower Brigade, like the black woman with the sign, were all victims of violence by citizens whom the society has failed. They have been exploited and led by the society to believe that they are worthless. Consequently, they are angry. In their own ways the people they attacked were reinforcing their feelings of worthlessness by demonstrating the ridiculousness of a parade supporting a disastrous war of aggression in Vietnam. Having been duped into believing anti-Communist propaganda, they felt that anyone who was not marching with them must have been a Communist or sympathetic to Communism at the very least.

In May 1970, during several of the mass demonstrations by students protesting the invasion of Cambodia, the killing of students by National Guardsmen at Kent State University in Ohio, and increased political repression throughout the

United States, high school and college students in New York City held daily demonstrations in the Wall Street area. On May 8 several hundred helmeted construction workers broke up the demonstration, injuring at least 70 persons. The student demonstration was nonviolent, but at about noon the crowd of construction workers, marching behind American flags, brushed the few policemen stationed there aside and charged the students. They used their helmets for weapons, and although it is estimated that they numbered about 200, they were reinforced by sympathetic bystanders eager to beat the demonstrators. Their rallying cry was, "Kill the Commie Bastards." From all reports, the police, who made no arrests, were "mingling amiably" with the construction workers while students were brutally beaten.

After leaving Wall Street the construction workers marched to City Hall. Enroute they ripped a Red Cross banner from the gates of Trinity Church, and attempted to remove the church flag, mistaking it for the flag of the National Liberation Front of South Vietnam. When they reached Pace College they invaded the building, breaking windows with clubs and crowbars, and beating any students they encountered.

At City Hall, the construction workers were angered because the flag there was flying at half-staff in honor of the four students killed at Kent State University. One of their numbers went to the roof and raised the flag again while others cheered wildly. When a member of the Mayor's staff again lowered the flag, the mob of construction workers reacted angrily, broke through police lines and stormed City Hall.

The police had been unable to curb the violence, they later maintained, because they were understaffed. However, the Police Department and the Mayor's office had both been warned by many telephone calls, including those from politicians and from construction workers who had attended planning meetings and were unsympathetic to the mob of super-patriots. Yet the police had not responded. The Mayor ordered an investigation of the incident, charging that New Yorkers had "witnessed a breakdown of the police as a barrier between them and wanton violence." Nearly four months later the police responded by issuing a 45-page report, defending their actions and extolling the virtues of the New York City Police Department for its "ability to conduct itself fairly and impartially in its manifold duties in the policing of Greater New York City and its multiplicity of citizens, and untold numbers of visitors, of all races, colors and creeds—religious and political."

The construction workers and bystanders who supported them in their violent rampage are ordinary citizens whose needs have not been met by the society. Although they may earn reasonable wages, their need for a sense of self-worth has not been realized. For them the students who demonstrate against the war represent a challenge, for the students say to them in many ways that they are fools. They say they are fools because they build the fortresses from which the privileged few make decisions which exploit them and the world's masses. They say they are fools to support a war geared to generate greater profits for the people whose sons and brothers manage to evade the draft, while they must work hard and long as their sons and brothers are killed in Vietnam. In short, the students say they are fools because they do not recognize the real source of their frustrations. This message gets through to the construction workers, and they react violently.

The war in Vietnam has served to enlighten those Americans too young to have been brainwashed in the early years of the Cold War to the aggressive nature of their country's foreign policy and the economic threat Communism poses.

Nevertheless, many older citizens remain firmly committed to belief in what is usually called the "evils of Communism," and while rabid anti-Communism is less prevalent today than it was in the 1950's, such a position is still virtually a prerequisite for political office in the United States. People who advocate more humane domestic and foreign policies continue to be labeled Communists. Anyone who favors peace in the world and social justice at home is still considered a Communist by most Americans. Those who oppose such acts as the sponsoring of invasions of Cuba and the economic boycott of that country, those who journey to Cuba to assist in harvesting sugar cane, those who protest the invasion of the Dominican Republic, those who oppose the domination of the United Nations by the United States and the governments it supports and maintains, those who advocate the admission of the People's Republic of China to the United Nations—all are believed to be traitors. Violence against such people is considered by many to be inherently correct, and the rulers of the nation sanction such an attitude because it serves to maintain the status quo.

In addition to these strongly entrenched feelings of anti-Communism, other social characteristics contribute to the violence in America. One such characteristic, obviously, is racism.

Racism

Violence against blacks and other racial minorities in the United States has always been extensive and is somehow considered to be qualitatively different from violence against white persons. Throughout much of American history, acts of brutality against blacks and Indians were either encouraged or ignored. As late as 1964, when three civil-rights workers were murdered by racists in Mississippi, this incident received international publicity because two of the three were white. In dragging the Mississippi River for their bodies, searchers found two unidentified blacks; one had been cut in half and the other beheaded. Since they were black, their murders had gone unnoticed, and one wonders how many others have met similar fates in the United States.

At South Carolina State College in Orangeburg, in Februrary 1968, three black students were killed and at least 28 others injured by highway patrolmen, while peacefully protesting the discriminatory practices of a local bowling alley. While their deaths were reported in the newspapers, they did not evoke the national outpouring which followed the killing of four white students at Kent State. Similarly, shortly after the events at Kent State, six black men were killed by the police in Augusta, Georgia, while protesting the treatment of juvenile prisoners in the county jail, one of whom had been killed. Each of the six was shot in the back. And at Jackson State College in Mississippi, one black high school student and one college student were murdered and nine others injured by state highway police, apparently without provocation. Neither student was even engaged in protest activities. The two happened to be present when the police opened fire into a crowd of students and into a women's dormitory. A policeman involved in the killings radioed to a hospital for assistance: "You better send some ambulances, we killed some niggers." These killings by the police were considered newsworthy but did not bring forth the shock and horror which followed the killing of four white students.

The killing of black people during the urban uprisings of the 1960's was widely reported in the media but usually considered justifiable homicide. At least 170 persons were killed and 6,500 wounded in the major uprisings in Los Angeles in 1965, in Cleveland in 1966, in Detroit and Newark in 1967, and in cities throughout the country after the assassination of Martin Luther King, Jr., in 1968. A vast majority of the people killed were black, and they were killed by law enforcement personnel, police and National Guardsmen, usually for such minor offenses as looting stores.

These killings resulted from threats to private property: that is, they were economic in origin. However, since those who were threatening the system were black, and since racism has attained a functional autonomy of its own, the slaughter of black people was facilitated.

The case of the American Indians parallels that of blacks, and in some respects violence against them has exceeded that against blacks. Since in recent years Indians have been reduced to a totally oppressed and isolated minority, and since their land has virtually all been confiscated, they have been relatively immune from the overt acts of violence to which blacks are so often subjected. As they move from reservations to large cities, however, they face the same racist violence blacks have encountered.

Of the other racial minorities, Mexican-Americans and Puerto Ricans have frequently been victims of overt racist violence. On the West Coast and in the Southwest, Mexican-Americans have faced collective violence in the form of riots against them, and they continue to be the victims of police brutality wherever they are located. As they organize themselves for protection against economic exploitation, they meet violence, and for those in the Southwest who demand that Mexican territory annexed by the United States be returned, brutality is commonplace. On the East Coast, because they are inclined to protest the injustices of American society, and since many of them support independence for their homeland, Puerto Ricans are frequently brutalized, often by the police. Many Puerto Rican organizations have adopted the tactics of black militants in demanding their rights, and they encounter the same acts of violence, especially police brutality. In the earlier years of immigration to the United States, Chinese and Japanese too met frequent violence. In large numbers they responded by isolating themselves from the larger society and withdrawing to sections of cities where they escape the violence white Americans insist upon inflicting on members of racial minorities.

Political dissenters have always been dealt with harshly, for they represent a threat to the basis of the society. Consequently, those active in movements for radical social change, regardless of ethnicity, have generated widespread violence on the part of those who would preserve the status quo. White youths who have rejected and resisted what they consider to be immoral features of the society and its foreign policy have assumed a status comparable to that of racial minorities, and force against them is encouraged. Hence, when they are killed or wounded by the police, National Guardsmen or construction workers, an elaborate mechanism of transfering the blame for the initiators of violence to its victims is set in motion. Protesting students burned down a building housing the Reserve Officers Training Corps on campus (an act of property destruction), and National Guardsmen were defended when they killed four of them. Residents of the town in which the university is located, along with other rank-and-file Americans, unhesitatingly expressed approval of the killings, and a special grand jury exonerated the killers and criticized their victims.

For members of racial minorities, or those who reject the assumptions of American society, life in the United States is difficult and cruel. For black people this is a three-and-one-half centuries' old story, and when blacks decide that they must do whatever is necessary to liberate themselves from oppression, they are met with force and condemnation. Those who are responsible for law enforcement seize upon the slightest provocation (real or imagined) to slaughter them in the streets, with the full realization that such behavior is much more likely to be rewarded than punished. The oppression of the Indians is an equally long story and in many respects a more brutal one.

Similar racist attitudes and behavior prevail toward Mexican-Americans and Puerto Ricans. More recently, white youths have joined the ranks of racial minorities as recipients of America's violence. Their resistance to the society's inhumanity and ruthlessness is so despised by frustrated and demoralized Americans that they, like nonwhites, are regarded as legitimate targets of violence.

Resistance to Change

A great deal of the violence in America results from the resistance of the society to reasoned demands for change. American society is basically conservative, and the country is ruled by a powerful central government which upholds the existing order. Any attempt to restructure the society along more humanitarian lines is resisted because the interests of the power elite are threatened. Those in positions of power and privilege have created what they consider to be the best of all possible worlds in the United States. They are amazed that some citizens would disagree with this judgment, and they usually dismiss dissidents as either sinister or naive. This view is probably shared by a vast majority of white citizens of all social classes, but not by many millions of others—blacks, college students and other young people, American Indians, Mexican-Americans, and Puerto Ricans. And as the true nature of the society is exposed to increasing numbers of citizens, movements for social change gain followers.

Since the society resists change, however, it follows that its approach to social problems is one of inaction, which leads to the compounding of problems until they reach crisis proportions. At the crisis point, it is somehow expected that poorly conceived crash measures will suffice to surmount the hurdle. This "muddling through" approach frequently serves to contain those advocating social change, but it is hardly a rational approach to the problems. When the proponents of social change become aware of this, they often intensify their demands, which leads to increasing polarization in the society, as manifested by the gap between nonwhite and white citizens and that between youth and their elders.

Because of the unresponsiveness of the society to reasoned criticism and demands for social change, individuals and groups with legitimate grievances are frequently driven to the point of employing force themselves. However, such force has usually been directed not against individuals but against property. Those who resist change, on the other hand, do not hesitate to apply force against individuals, and this is a difference of considerable magnitude. It is one thing to burn a branch of the Bank of America to the ground, or to bomb an empty office building, but it is quite another to kill and maim people. Since the demand for profits is the *sine qua non* of our capitalist system, the destruction of banks or other real property strikes at the very foundation of the system, and individuals involved in these acts are dealt with swiftly and harshly. On the other hand, the killing of individuals who advocate social change strengthens rather than weakens the system.

Social conditions in the United States have reached a point where concerned individuals feel that the only method available for redress of legitimate grievances is that of direct confrontation with those responsible for the maintenance of a society which works against the best interests of human beings. Years of peaceful efforts in the civil-rights movement finally succeeded in achieving legal equality *in principle* for black people, but the relative status of blacks and whites in reality remained much as it had been. Black people thereupon turned to militancy and property destruction. After the several black uprisings in the second half of the 1960's, greater changes in the status of black people were accomplished in a few years than in 100 years of peaceful protest.

Shortly after sections of Los Angeles, Newark, and Detroit went up in flames, it was felt that if concessions to blacks were not forthcoming, the flames would engulf the entire society. Those who had been responsible for the oppression of black people suddenly realized that they could move to ameliorate the conditions producing such outpourings of anger. Owners of private industries soon discovered that many of the positions which had traditionally been reserved for white people could adequately be filled by blacks. Perhaps more than others, educational institutions moved swiftly to correct past injustices. The result was that the enrollment of black students in colleges and universities doubled between 1965 and 1970.

Once civil rights activities reached the point where virtually all legal discrimination against blacks was eradicated, many white youths transferred their efforts to the peace movement. They peacefully petitioned the government to end the killing of Asians, but their appeals fell on deaf ears. Realizing that American society responds more favorably to threats to its structure than to appeals to reason, they too moved to a position of confrontation with those responsible for maintaining what they considered to be policies directed against the preservation of human life.

These advocates of social change at first appealed to reason before resorting to policies of confrontation and force against property. The opponents of social change, on the other hand, responded to such protests by engaging in acts of violence against the protesters. If the society had been responsive to reasoned appeals for change, much of the property damage and attendant violence against persons could have been averted. But few changes in American history have resulted from appeals to reason.

On the national level, it was only after thousands of children had been killed in factories that child labor laws were enacted. Thousands of persons were killed and injured before workers were permitted to organize themselves into unions. Also, it was only after students occupied buildings and brought some universities to a halt that minor higher educational reforms were initiated. Given the long history of tragedies and confrontations necessary before even minor social changes are instituted, it is not surprising that groups of citizens feel impelled to force such changes by confronting those responsible for maintaining a society in which social justice is a privilege, not a right. Nor is it surprising that when these confrontations occur, the protesters meet acts of violence from those opposed to social change.

In addition to the foregoing, there are no doubt many other factors in American culture which contribute to the tradition of violence. For example, throughout the country statues and monuments are erected to soldiers and others who are honored for acts of violence. Indeed, the great culture heroes of the society are among the most violent men it has produced. There is in this country a widespread fascination with the most violent sports, such as boxing and football. In serious American literature, writers have persistently used homicidal violence and rape as major themes. Policemen are invariably rewarded for engaging in armed confrontations. Similarly, servicemen are presented medals based on the number of the "enemy" they kill. These practices are not uniquely American, but they are deeply rooted in the United States and flow from its long history of violence.

Given these cultural characteristics, it is not surprising that America is one of the most violent societies in the world. Indeed, individuals who manage somehow to respect the precept of nonviolence in spite of these compelling forces and the country's violent history are the exception, not the rule. For they, rather than the violent ones, are deviants in a society where violent behavior is the norm.

VII

►►►►►►

The Future of Violence in America

Is the United States likely to become more violent in the future, or is violent behavior likely to decline? What factors will contribute to an increase or decline in violent behavior among Americans? The assumption must be made that since the level of violence this society has experienced throughout its history is not a function of innate aggressiveness on the part of the American people, it is possible to reduce and even eradicate such expressions of aggression. That is, since violence is learned behavior, it can also be unlearned. But violence, like many other forms of human behavior, is more easily learned than unlearned. Some societies have managed to transform themselves from relatively violent states into ones in which acts of violence are rare. In order for such a transformation to take place, however, the social climate must be one in which violent behavior is no longer rewarded.

American society is in a state of chaos; it has reached the breaking point. For the first time in its history, there is real alienation among citizens and widespread feeling that institutions, most notably the Federal Government, have failed the people. Furthermore, the society is divided into two hostile camps: those who demand radical change and those who seek to maintain the status quo. In the first category are to be found millions of people under 25 years of age, who comprise the so-called counter culture, as well as blacks and other racial minorities. Their opponents are mainly middle- and working-class whites over the age of 25, who are frequently called the silent majority.

The silent majority is typified by the construction workers ("hardhats") who brutalize those who protest against the country's domestic and foreign policies, and who are rewarded for such behavior by being invited to the White House to receive the praise of a grateful President. In an interview with Joe Kelly, one of the construction workers who participated in the attack on peace demonstrators in New York's financial district, Richard Rogin presented in the *New York Times Magazine* a picture of this kind of citizen.

Joe Kelly, whose plastic construction helmet is decorated with flag decals and "FOR GOD AND COUNTRY," is a 31-year-old college dropout. He is an elevator construction mechanic, a highly skilled occupation, at the World Trade Center in New York. The father of three children, he lives with his family in half of a $40,000 two-family house, which he owns on Staten Island.

A devout Roman Catholic, Joe Kelly grew up on Staten Island, to which his mother immigrated from Ireland. His father, who was born in New York, died of a heart attack in

1959. He went to parochial school on Staten Island, where he was mainly interested in athletics. While in high school he delivered newspapers and worked in a drug store. After graduation he went off to St. Peter's College in Jersey City on a basketball scholarship, but soon lost interest in his studies, and after one year withdrew.

He then worked briefly as a seaman on oil tankers, and as a member of a crew automating elevators, before he was drafted into the Army. As a soldier he says he enjoyed the regimented life in the Army. After serving for two years as a military policeman, he returned to elevator service and installation work, married a local girl and started raising a family.

While Joe Kelly earns between $15,000 and $18,000 a year because of overtime work, and rents out the other half of his house for $200 a month, he is forced to supplement his income by working three nights a week as a bartender. He attends Mass every Sunday and coaches basketball and baseball teams in the local parish. He has been unable to take his family on vacation in the summers because of expenses connected with the house. For entertainment he takes his wife to the movies about once every six weeks.

His reading matter is limited to the New York *Daily News,* the sports pages of the New York *Post,* and *Popular Mechanics Magazine*. When asked to account for his strong anti-Communist beliefs, he attributed them to his admiration for the late Senator Joseph McCarthy. In 1964 he voted for Barry Goldwater for President and in 1968, Richard Nixon. He admires the movie actor John Wayne, Vice President Spiro Agnew, and Mayor Richard Daley of Chicago. He is adamantly opposed to having a black family move to his street because he feels this would cause a decline in the value of his property. He equates the office of President of the United States and the head of the Roman Catholic Church: "The Pope to the Catholic Church is the same as the President to the American people. He's the one who decides."

Although Joe Kelly says he is opposed to violence because it "doesn't solve a damn thing," he admits that during the peace demonstrations he became enraged and struck a student, whereupon "He went down, I know that, and I just figured he wouldn't be back for more." He is infuriated about the life style and activities of college students and is convinced that they are dupes of subversive teachers who are under the control of foreign Communist powers. The magnitude, frequency and nature of the peace demonstrations pushed him to the "boiling point," for he is proud of his patriotism: "I guess the average construction worker is what you would call a flag waver. You can call me a flag-waver any day of the week. I think that's something to be proud of, to be a flag-waver, to be proud of your country." He feels that what America needs at the present time is more "law and order."

Millions of Americans, like Joe Kelly, have been pushed to the boiling point. While they acknowledge that the country is in a state of disorder, they see it as a temporary phenomenon brought about by those determined to destroy the American way, especially rebellious youth, blacks and other racial minorities. These citizens are usually hard-working, scrupulous, reverent of authority, and devoted to their loved ones. But they are also violent, and in their anger they are willing to slaughter others or see them killed in support of what they see as the virtues of the traditional American system. For example, a Mississippi physician wrote a letter to his son, who was entering Tulane University in the fall of 1970, cautioning him against participating in disruptive activities. In the letter, which was reprinted in the *New York Times,* he informed his son that if his advice should be ignored and his death resulted, "Mother and I will grieve but we will gladly buy dinner for the National Guardsman who shot you."

For centuries, citizens like Joe Kelly have been taught the virtue of hard work. Millions of immigrants left Europe for North America attempting to improve themselves and create a better life for their children. And while many of them have no doubt improved their economic status in the United States, compared to their relatives who remained elsewhere, the struggle has been hard. Joe Kelly's father died of a heart attack at the age of 45. And although his earnings as a construction worker are substantial, he must still depend on overtime, a second job and the rental of half of his house in order to provide "something nice for the wife and kids, someplace where the kids could grow up and have their own backyard."

In addition to having virtually no time for relaxation, Kelly faces frustrating uncertainties connected with working in the construction industry. The building of the World Trade Center in New York provided the opportunity for substantial overtime, thereby increasing his earnings, but there is no certainty that a similar opportunity will be available once the complex has been completed. There is always the possibility that he will be forced to abandon the "safety" of his all-white neighborhood.

The millions of Americans who either brutalize others or sanction such behavior become enraged when today's youth eagerly display contempt for values their elders have lived by. A strong fear of Communism is added to their other anxieties, justifying their demands for a strong central government, even a fascist dictatorship. They enthusiastically cheer the Vice President when he rails against "the whole damn zoo" of "deserters, malcontents, radicals, incendiaries, and the civil and uncivil disobedients," and suggests that they be separated from society like "rotten apples from a barrel." Furthermore, they support any politician who promises substantial doses of repression. What they appear to be saying is that only a fascist dictatorship can restore the American way. In short, they are the citizens former Chief Justice of the Supreme Court Earl Warren has suggested would reject the Bill of Rights if it was submitted to a referendum.

Millions of youth, on the other hand, have developed a radically different perception of the world, a new consciousness, in the terminology of Charles A. Reich in his *The Greening of America*. These young people have rejected the society and what they see as its real characteristics: racism, aggressive warfare, hunger, unresponsive government, and the general debasement of the quality of life. In place of these they seek new values, new goals and a new awareness. Since most of them were born after World War II, they are too young to have been indoctrinated into hysterical fear of Communism during the height of the Cold War.

Many of them were involved in the peace and civil-rights movements of the late 1960's. It was through such activities as these, and the political campaign of Senator Eugene McCarthy in 1968, that most of them realized the futility of peaceful protest. Some of them have elected to escape the oppressiveness of life in America by joining the subculture of drugs and rock music, but also by seeking communal living, affirmation of self, respect for others and openness to new experiences. Their model for this kind of consciousness (which Reich calls "Consciousness III") was the Woodstock Music and Art Fair, held in Sullivan County, New York, in August 1969. A total of some 500,000 young people attended this event for three days, and in spite of shortages of food, water and sanitary facilities, as well as other inconveniences, an extraordinary spirit of love, cooperation and peacefulness permeated the event. Violence was absent. For a brief three days Woodstock generated an atmosphere of community, a feeling of being in liberated territory, far away from the battlefields of American cities.

Reich feels that a new attitude toward life is spreading in America, most rapidly among the youth, but also among some of their elders. He considers the spread of this new consciousness to be a revolutionary development more profound than any in modern history: "Beside it, a mere revolution, such as the French or the Russian, seems inconsequential—a mere shift in the base of power." Among the Consciousness III people there is a new reverence for life and love, and a concomitant rejection of violence. Indeed, Reich feels that the revolution they are making will radically alter the structure of the society without violence: "It will not require violence to succeed, and it cannot be successfully resisted by violence." He sees it as a mass act of personal liberation, not a struggle for power among competing groups.

The notion of an impending revolution without violence is no doubt comforting to most Americans, but violence is institutionalized in America. And American violence is no more likely to exempt those who manage to liberate themselves from older perceptions of reality than any who threaten established authority. Historically, most violence in America has been aggressive rather than defensive, and while Reich's youths might not initiate such behavior, there is no guarantee they will not be its victims. The millions of Americans typified by the construction worker Joe Kelly and the Mississippi physician, angry and terrified of these youths, would either kill them or reward the National Guard for their murders.

Furthermore, although the present system may have been weakened by the revolution in consciousness, it is not likely to collapse. Indeed, there is a tendency toward greater concentration of power in the hands of the Federal Government. And the law can be used against the youth whenever it is decided that they seriously threaten the system, as was done with the Indians and is currently the case with the Black Panthers. In addition, many youths who develop elements of the new consciousness are soon coopted by the system after they graduate from school. Some of them have worked recently for such a conservative political candidate as Senator James Buckley of New York.

Many of the superficial elements of the youth culture, such as hair styles, music and dress have spread to the larger society. But there is no evidence that these have altered the basic values of its members. On the other hand, colleges and universities have been significantly affected by the new consciousness. Fraternities and sororities are experiencing difficulty surviving on campuses, while radical activities and groups are thriving. The first nationwide student strike in American history, affecting some 760 colleges and universities, occurred after the American invasion of Cambodia. Students at Yale University forced the school to close out of solidarity with the leader of the Black Panther Party, who was being tried in the courts of New Haven, a trial believed by many to have been simply another act of persecution of members of the Party. Princeton University in 1970 awarded an honorary degree to Bob Dylan, a symbol of the new consciousness. Throughout the country students have succeeded in forcing academic institutions to relinquish ties to military- and war-related industries and to concern themselves with more humanitarian projects. For the first time in history, 1970 commencement programs featured anti-war and feminist speakers, while representatives of the Federal Government, previously in demand as commencement speakers, received few invitations.

But these are hardly revolutionary changes, and there is no evidence that the message of the new consciousness has affected Joe Kelly and others like him, except to make them angry. Moreover, as a result of the slow pace with which change has come about, many in the youth movement have rejected peaceful dissent in favor of direct confrontation. This tactic stimulates repression and violence, forcing still others to conclude that the only recourse which remains is for them to demonstrate their convictions through acts of property destruction.

The destruction of property is repeatedly judged by Americans to be a more serious offense than destroying people, especially if those people are Asians, blacks or, to an increasing degree, youthful white dissenters. The burning down of a Bank of America building by students at the University of California at Santa Barbara in February 1970 brought a chorus of disapproval from around the country, while the killing of one student and injuring of hundreds more by the police and National Guardsmen in the same demonstration raised few voices in protest, other than those of students. Whenever students are killed or injured in protest demonstrations, and at least 14 were killed between 1962 and the end of the school year in 1970, if property is destroyed the destruction of property is invariably seen by most Americans as the more serious offense.

Youthful dissidents have learned that in materialistic America, the destruction of property forces the leaders to at least realize the seriousness of the problems facing the society. They are not unaware that the black uprisings of the 1960's so frightened Americans that some concessions were made. And as with blacks, the major thrust of their destruction has been property, not people. Although some writers have suggested that the bombing of buildings is the work of demented minds, a much more likely explanation is that these young people have despaired of changing the society through peaceful protest. The recent bombings are in fact acts of desperation.

During 1969 and 1970 the revolutionary left accelerated its bombing campaign in cities throughout the country. Even so, aside from the accidental explosion in New York's Greenwich Village which killed three persons assumed to be members of the Weathermen, an off-shoot of Students for a Democratic Society, the bombings have killed or injured very few persons. The bombers have tried to make sure that buildings would be evacuated before the bombs exploded. For example, in November 1969, when explosives were set off in the New York offices of Chase Manhattan Bank, General Motors, and Standard Oil of New Jersey, guards and news offices were telephoned in advance to insure that the buildings would be cleared of people. Similarly, in March 1970, before explosives were set off in the offices of General Telephone and Electronics, International Business Machines and Socony Mobil, the New York Police Department received a telephone call which warned: "Listen closely. At about 1:40 A.M. bombs will explode at all of these addresses: At 150 East 42nd Street, at 730 Third Avenue, and at 425 Park Avenue. Evacuate everyone from these buildings." At the appointed time, the explosions occurred.

On both these occasions, groups of underground revolutionaries claimed credit for the bombings in letters to the news media and explained why they had resorted to such actions. In the November 1969 bombings, the letter included the following: "The Vietnam war is only the most obvious evidence of the way this country's power destroys people. The giant corporations of America have now spread themselves all over the world, forcing entire foreign economies into total dependence on American money and goods." And the letter sent after the March 1970 bombings, by a group calling itself "Revolutionary Force 9," declared: "IBM, Mobile and GTE are enemies of all life. In 1969 IBM made $250 million, Mobile $150 million and GTE $140 million for US 'defense' contracts—profits made from the suffering and deaths of human beings. All three profit not only from death in Vietnam but also from Amerikan imperialism in all of the Third World. They profit from racist oppression of black, Puerto Rican and other minority colonies outside Amerika, from the suffering and death of men in the Amerikan army, from sexism, from the exploitation and degradation of employees forced into lives of anti-human work, from the pollution and destruction of our environment."

The letter ended with the following: "This way of 'life' is a way of death. To work for the industries of death is to murder. To know of the torments Amerika inflicts on the Third World, but not to sympathize and identify, is to deny our own humanity. It is to deny our right to love—and not to love is to die. We refuse. In death-directed Amerika there is only one way to a life of love and freedom: to attack and destroy the forces of death and exploitation and to build a just society—revolution."

The revolutionary left has focused its bombings on symbolic targets, those it sees as responsible for destruction abroad and dehumanization at home. These have included Reserve Officers Training Corps buildings, corporate offices, police stations, military research centers, and other organizations associated with the military. In addition to the explosions at the headquarters of the three corporations, in 1969 alone, hundreds of bombs and other explosives were set off throughout the country, including 93 in New York City. Targets included the offices of the United Fruit Company, banks, draft induction centers and local draft board offices, department stores, and the offices of several other large corporations. Several people suffered injuries, but no deaths were recorded. On the other hand, property damage —the purpose of the explosions—was extensive.

In the first three months of 1970 the bombings accelerated. The targets were similar: several police stations, including those in New York and San Francisco; barracks at the Oakland, California Army base for use by soldiers enroute to Vietnam; ROTC buildings at the University of Colorado, the University of Michigan, the University of Wisconsin, Texas A and M University, Washington University in St. Louis, and the University of Oregon; Selective Service offices; National Guard armories; and the headquarters of General Telephone and Electronics, IBM and Socony Mobil Oil Company, all of which are engaged in war research.

After the invasion of Cambodia and the killing of students at Kent State University and Jackson State College, in May 1970, National Guard armories and ROTC buildings were the targets of arson and fire bombings at colleges and universities which had previously experienced little if any disruptions. In addition to buildings directly related to the military, university buildings such as gymnasiums, administration buildings, student centers and book stores were damaged or destroyed throughout the country, and the magnitude and number of these incidents make it unlikely that they could have been the work of a small band of underground revolutionaries. Many students who had not previously been involved in such acts of terrorism were apparently so outraged by the turn of events that they felt impelled to demonstrate their revulsion in the only manner sure to be understood by America's leaders. There are indications that a growing number of students view bombings and arson as a legitimate response to a heedless and insensitive government.

In attempting to cope with the bombings and burnings, the Federal Government has accelerated its surveillance of radical groups and individuals but has elected to ignore the conditions which precipitated the crisis. The President has called the young revolutionaries "young criminals posturing as romantic revolutionaries," and one of his consultants has commented that "Some of these kids don't know what country this is. They think it's Bolivia." Consequently, no attempt is made to ameliorate the conditions which provoked the acts of desperation. According to the *New York Times,* the Administration has concluded that it is as futile to attempt to bring these disenchanted youth back into the mainstream of society "as turning off the radio in the middle of a ball game to try to change the score." And a highly placed assistant to the President added, "We're dealing with the criminal mind, with people who have snapped for some reason."

In hearings by the Senate Permanent Investigations Committee, in July 1970, the mayor of Seattle advocated killing those who are convicted of bombings. He testified that the incidence of bombings in his city had declined when the police shot and killed a young black man whom they suspected of planting a dynamite bomb near a white-owned real estate office. The mayor said, "I suspect killing a person involved in a bombing . . . might be somewhat of a deterrent."

With such attitudes on the part of public officials, the likelihood is that the activities of youthful revolutionaries will multiply and that increasing numbers of them will go underground. The technique of kidnapping foreign diplomats and holding them hostage in order to force concessions from an unresponsive government, as practiced by revolutionaries in Latin America, may well be adopted by youthful revolutionaries in the United States. And in response to such a development, repression would accelerate, as well as violence from the silent majority.

Thus the crisis posed by the deep split among Americans is a serious one. Each opposing faction is determined to resolve the present state of chaos in its own way. Those who hold economic and political power concede that some aspects of the society are in need of reform, but they are unwilling to permit changes which would alter the structure of the society in any fundamental way. And in this opposition they have the strong support of the majority of Americans. Violence on a wide scale appears therefore to be inevitable, for the proponents of radical social change are equally adamant.

During the 1960's several federal commissions were appointed to investigate various aspects of violence in America. In addition to the National Commission on the Causes and Prevention of Violence, there was the Warren Commission on the assassination of President John F. Kennedy, the Crime Commission, and the Kerner Commission on civil disorders. Although these were primarily political bodies, some of their reports were perceptive and wide-ranging in their analysis of the social forces causing violent behavior. Yet the recommendations in these reports were either ignored or dismissed by public officials, including the Presidents who commissioned them. This is of course characteristic of the American approach to social problems, which are usually ignored in the hope that they will somehow disappear.

America is not the only society in which violence has been a salient component of the experience of its people, nor is it likely to be the last. One of the most depressing features of history is its saturation with acts of cruelty and barbarism by human beings toward one another, to the extent that such behavior appears to have been a normal part of human relationships from the beginning. The pessimists who prophesy a bloody future for mankind clearly have greater historical evidence to support their prognosis than those who are optimistic about the future course of human history.

Further, American society has not been the most bloody on record, but it has been one in which violent behavior has played a central role in the resolution of conflict since its birth. On the other hand, there is much in the American experience which reflects a healthy respect for human life and dignity. Perhaps no development in history so clearly affirms these values as the contemporary youth movement, with its rejection of racism and other forms of dehumanization at home and aggressive warfare abroad. It is unfortunate that so many Americans reject this message, having been for so long exposed to a culture which has thrived on death and human destruction.

The world has changed radically since World War II, and the current generation of youth is aware of the distortions of fact that have been passed on to them by their elders, and that continue to be recited by the leaders of their government. Through modern communications media, young people have been made conscious of the struggles for greater freedom and self-determination by oppressed peoples the world over, and it is not surprising that they would identify with the oppressed. Furthermore, since the use of force has played such a key role in the resolution of conflict in American history, it is understandable that young people today should resort to force when other appeals for change are ignored.

The 17-year-old black youth in California who smuggled several pistols and a carbine into the Marin County Courthouse on August 7, 1970, leading to a shootout in which he was killed along with two prisoners and a Superior Court judge, took this way of striking at his country's system of justice. At the time, his older brother and two other black inmates were being held in Soledad Prison on a charge of murdering a white guard. Several days before the guard was killed, three unarmed black prisoners had been killed by another white guard during a minor racial skirmish. The District Attorney and a grand jury ruled that the killing of the three blacks was justifiable homicide but the later killing of the white guard was an act of retaliation, and the three black prisoners were charged with murder. Fearing that his brother would be sentenced to die, the 17-year-old youth attempted to hold the judge and several jurors as hostages in order to save his brother's life.

The action of this youth indicates a loss of faith in the possibility of securing justice for black people in America. The revolutionary youths who claim credit for bombing buildings have also lost faith in American justice and defend their actions as necessary to secure desired ends. While their acts of terrorism have not been aimed at human beings, with elaborate and generally successful procedures worked out to avoid deaths and injuries, on a few occasions deaths and injuries have resulted. Such was the case at the University of Wisconsin on August 23, 1970, when an explosion at the Army Mathematics Research Center killed a post-doctoral student and injured four other persons. And the increase in acts of terrorism will no doubt lead to additional bloodshed.

It is often claimed that violence is an ineffective means of resolving conflict, but the history of the United States demonstrates that in fact many social disputes have been settled by violent means. The future of violence in the United States depends, in large measure, on the willingness of the country's leaders to reorder its priorities both at home and abroad. Policies of repression against certain segments of the population can only serve to aggravate the problem. Violent behavior is not limited to certain categories of citizens; it is a national problem which includes persons in all social categories. The criminologists who embrace the view that violence is largely limited to specific subcultures within a generally nonviolent society are contributing to the cultural myth of nonviolence. These scholars simply separate acts of violence into sociological categories—race or ethnicity, age, geographical location, social class, etc. But to do this merely obscures the fact that such behavior is not peculiar to a subgroup of people but is a reflection of the dominant values of the society as a whole. While middle-class people may give verbal support to the notion of nonviolence, they at the same time either surreptitiously participate in violent acts or endorse them on the part of others.

While the poor in general and members of ethnic minorities in particular may show a disproportionately high rate of violent crime, they are hardly responsible for the acts of mass brutality which have characterized so much of American history. Furthermore, they are hardly responsible for the massive slaughter of people in Vietnam, although they are frequently forced into participating in such acts. Nor are they responsible for the conditions in the society which have nurtured violent behavior. Since so-called subcultures of violence invariably include members of racial minorities, it has been asserted that these people deviate from the norms of middle-class white society. It seems more likely that they reflect a well-established cultural pattern of violence, often in exaggerated form.

Because of our long history of violence, and the social values which condone such behavior, the likelihood of domestic tranquility in the near future is not great. America is basically conservative, and justice for many citizens has never been achieved. Along with oppressed peoples throughout the world, large segments of the American population are now demanding justice and an end to the general debasement of life in the society. It is difficult for one to maintain his humanity in the United States as it is now structured. That Americans can view the destruction of peasants in Asia on the evening's television news reports, enjoy their dinner and retire to their bedrooms for a serene night's sleep, all of which is made possible by the exploitation of a grossly disproportionate share of the earth's resources, indicates a loss of humanity. Americans permit their leaders to commit atrocities in their name. A more humane people would demand of their government that the killing and destruction cease, and the more sensitive citizens, particularly the youth, are making just this demand.

Given the strong resistance of the society to fundamental social change, which even some government officials concede is a prerequisite for domestic tranquility, the likelihood is that the 1970's will be at least as violent as the 1960's. Some of the more affluent citizens might escape the full force of American violence, especially violent crime, by taking refuge in what the National Commission on the Causes and Prevention of violence has called "safe areas," sealed off from the slums and patrolled by heavily armed guards, but no security precautions can be wholly effective. Our political assassinations and the frequent bombing even of heavily guarded police stations serve as proof that all Americans are vulnerable to acts of violence.

While violence has been an integral component of the American experience, and while Americans are among the most violent of all people at the present time, it does not follow that such behavior derives from the inherent character of the people. Like many others, Americans have learned their behavior as members of a society which nurtures coercion and cruelty. Since it is learned, violent behavior can be modified, but only if the climate of the society is supportive of such a change.

At the present time most Americans will blindly support any politician who promises more repression against those they see as responsible for the present disorder in the society. They are frustrated and angry, and rebellious youth and racial minorities are the targets of their frustrated, angry assault. Although they attribute much of the chaos in America to the permissiveness of the society, it is they who have been too permissive with their government. They have allowed the creation of powerful central government which supports wealth and privilege through the use of force. And they demand even greater regimentation by their government. Their cries for more repression may be answered, but repression will generate even greater violence, for the revolutionary youth are determined that America be transformed into a livable society. In any case, the future of violence in America is not reassuring.

References

I. Introduction: On Violence in America

Robert Ardrey, *African Genesis,* New York: Dell Publishing Co., 1967.

———, *The Territorial Imperative,* New York: Atheneum Publishers, 1966.

Jason Epstein, *The Great Conspiracy Trial,* New York: Random House, 1970.

Konrad Lorenz, *On Aggression,* New York: Harcourt, Brace and World, 1966.

M. F. Ashley Montagu (ed.), *Man and Aggression,* New York: Oxford University Press, 1968.

National Commission on the Causes and Prevention of Violence, *Rights in Conflict: The Chicago Police Riot*, New York: New American Library, 1968.

Arthur Schlesinger, Jr., *Violence: America in the Sixties,* New York: New American Library, 1968.

II. The Prevalence of Violence

Lester Adelson, "Slaughter of Innocents — A Study of Forty-Six Homicides in which the Victims were Children," *New England Journal of Medicine,* Vol. 264 (1961), 1345–49.

James K. Batten, "You Must Be Out of Your Mind to be Out Alone After Dark in a Neighborhood Like This," *New York Times Magazine* (March 22, 1970), pp. 22–23, 60–89.

Robert V. Bruce, *1877: Year of Violence,* Indianapolis and New York: Bobbs-Merrill Co., 1959.

Robert Coles, "Terror Struck Children," *The New Republic* (May 20, 1964), pp. 11–13.

The Congressional Record, Vol. 115, No. 103 (June 23, 1969), pp. 16839–16844.

Howard G. Earl, "10,000 Children Battered and Starved, Hundreds Die," *Today's Health* (September 1965), pp. 24–31.

Vincent J. Esposito (ed.), *The West Point Atlas of American Wars,* New York: Frederick A. Praeger, 1959.

Federal Bureau of Investigation, *Uniform Crime Reports,* Washington: Government Printing Office, 1969.

David G. Gil, "Incidence of Child Abuse and Demographic Characteristics of Persons Involved," in Ray E. Helfer and C. Henry Kempe (eds.), *The Battered Child,* Chicago: University of Chicago Press, 1968, pp. 19–40.

Ray E. Helfer and C. Henry Kempe (eds.), *The Battered Child,* Chicago: University of Chicago Press, 1968.

Vernon H. Jensen, *Heritage of Conflict,* Ithaca, N.Y.: Cornell University Press, 1950.

C. Henry Kempe, Frederic N. Silverman, Brandt F. Steele, William Droegemuller, and Henry K. Silver, "The Battered Child Syndrome," *Journal of the American Medical Association,* Vol. 181 (1962), pp. 17–24.

National Commission on the Causes and Prevention of Violence, *Firearms and Violence in American Life,* Washington: Government Printing Office, 1969.

National Commission on the Causes and Prevention of Violence, *To Establish Justice, to Insure Domestic Tranquility,* Washington: Government Printing Office, 1969.

New York Times (April 9, 1969), pp. 1, 12.

President's Commission on Law Enforcement and Administration of Justice, *The Challenge of Crime in A Free Society,* Washington: Government Printing Office, 1967.

Steven V. Roberts, "Los Angeles Area is Shaken over a Series of Violent Acts," *New York Times* (May 3, 1970), p. 71.

Philip Taft, *Organized Labor in American History,* New York: Harper and Row, 1964.

Philip Taft and Philip Ross, "American Labor Violence: Its Causes, Character, and Outcome," in Hugh D. Graham and Ted R. Gurr (eds.), *The History of Violence in America,* New York: Bantam Books, 1969, pp. 281–395.

U.S. News and World Report (August 4, 1969), pp. 47–48.

George P. West, *Report on the Colorado Strike,* Washington: Commission on Industrial Relations, 1915.

Leontine Young, *Wednesday's Children: A Study of Child Neglect and Abuse,* New York: McGraw-Hill, 1964.

III. Violence in International Relations: Vietnam, An American Atrocity

Harry Ashmore and William C. Baggs, *Mission to Hanoi,* New York: G. Putnam's Sons, 1968.

Malcolm W. Browne, *The New Face of War,* Indianapolis and New York: Bobbs-Merrill Co., 1968.

Wilfred G. Burchett, *Vietnam North,* New York: International Publishers, 1966.

Raymond R. Coffey, "The Pinkville Massacre: Why It Could Happen," *Chicago Daily News* (November 26, 1969), p. 4.

Donald Duncan, *The New Legions,* New York: Random House, 1967.

Bernard Fall, "Blitz in Vietnam," *The New Republic* (October 9, 1965), pp. 17–21.

John Gerassi, *North Vietnam: A Documentary,* Indianapolis and New York: Bobbs-Merrill, 1968.

Richard Hammer, *One Morning in the War,* New York: Coward-McCann, 1970.

Frank Harvey, *Air War–Vietnam,* New York: Bantam Books, 1967.

Seymour Hersh, *My Lai 4,* New York: Random House, 1970.

In the Name of America, New York: Clergy and Laymen Concerned About Vietnam, 1968.

Victor Knoebl, *Victor Charlie,* New York: Frederick Praeger, 1967.

Mark Lane, *Conversations With Americans,* New York: Simon and Schuster, 1970.

Jack Langguth, "The War in Vietnam Can be Won—But," *New York Times Magazine* (September 19, 1965), pp. 30–31.

Michael Maclear, "Inside North Vietnam," *Chicago Daily News* (November 10–13, 1969), pp. 1–2.

Mary McCarthy, *Vietnam,* New York: Harcourt Brace and World, 1967.

Charles C. Mokcos, "Why Men Fight," *Transaction,* Vol. 7, No. 1 (November 1969), pp. 13–23.

The New Yorker (December 20, 1969), p. 27.

Newsweek (November 29, 1965), pp. 21–23.

William F. Pepper, "The Children of Vietnam," *Ramparts* (January 1967), pp. 44–68.

James H. Pickerell, *Vietnam in the Mud,* Indianapolis and New York: Bobbs-Merrill, 1966.

Norman Poirier, "An American Atrocity," *Esquire* (August 1969), pp. 59–63, ff.

Bertrand Russell, *War Crimes in Vietnam,* New York: Monthly Review Press, 1967.

Harrison E. Salisbury, *Behind the Lines–Hanoi,* New York: Harper and Row, 1967.

Jonathan Schell, *The Village of Ben Suc,* New York: Alfred A. Knopf, 1967.

Neil Sheehan, "When The Rains Came to Vietnam," *New York Times Magazine* (June 14, 1964), pp. 12–13, ff.

Desmond Smith, "There Must Have Been Easier Wars," *The Nation* (June 12, 1967), pp. 746–47.

Benjamin Spock and Mitchell Zimmerman, *Dr. Spock on Vietnam,* New York: Dell Publishing Co., 1968.

Telford Taylor, *Nuremberg and Vietnam: An American Tragedy,* Chicago: Quadrangle Books, 1970.

William Tuhoy, "A Big 'Dirty Little War,'" *New York Times Magazine* (November 28, 1965), pp. 43, ff.

IV. Violence in Domestic Relations: Persecution of Black and Red People

Ralph K. Andrist, *The Long Death: The Last Days of the Plains Indians,* New York: Macmillan, 1964.

William Brandon, *The American Heritage Book of Indians,* New York: Dell Publishing Company, 1964.

B. A. Botkin, *Lay My Burden Down,* Chicago: University of Chicago Press, 1945.

Chicago Commission on Race Relations, *The Negro in Chicago,* Chicago: University of Chicago Press, 1922.

John Collier, *Indians of the Americas,* New York: New American Library, 1947.

John Hope Franklin, *From Slavery to Freedom,* New York: Alfred A. Knopf, 1948.

————, *The Militant South,* Boston: Beacon Press, 1964.

Ralph Ganzburg, *100 Years of Lynchings,* New York: Lancer Books, 1962.

Helen Hunt Jackson, *A Century of Dishonor,* New York: Harper and Brothers, 1881.

Guy B. Johnson, "Patterns of Race Conflict," in Edgar T. Thompson (ed.), *Race Relations and the Race Problem,* Durham, N.C.: Duke University Press, 1939, pp. 125–151.

Alvin M. Josephy, Jr., *The Indian Heritage of America,* New York: Alfred A. Knopf, 1968.

Alfred McClung Lee and Norman D. Humphrey, *Race Riot,* New York: The Dryden Press, 1943.

Lynchings and What they Mean, Atlanta, Ga.: Southern Commission on the Study of Lynching, 1931.

John G. Neihardt, *Black Elk Speaks,* Lincoln, Neb.: University of Nebraska Press, 1961.

Francis Parkman, *The Conspiracy of Pontiac and the Indian War,* Boston: Little, Brown and Co., 1879.

Howard H. Peckham, *Pontiac and the Indian Uprising,* Chicago: University of Chicago Press, 1947.

Henry A. Poski and Roscoe C. Brown, Jr., *The Negro Almanac,* New York: Bellwether Publishing Co., 1967.

Arthur F. Raper, *The Tragedy of Lynching,* Chapel Hill: University of North Carolina Press, 1933.

Elliott M. Rudwick, *Race Riot at East St. Louis, July 2, 1917,* Cleveland: World Publishing Co., 1966.

Mari Sandoz, *Cheyenne Autumn,* New York: Avon Books, 1964.

Robert Shogan and Tom Craig, *The Detroit Riot,* Philadelphia, Chilton Books, 1964.

Irving J. Sloan, *Our Violent Past,* New York: Random House, 1970.

Kenneth Stampp, *The Peculiar Institution,* New York: Vintage Books, 1956.

Tuskegee Institute, *1926 Negro Year Book*, New York: William A. Wise and Co., 1925.

Arthur I. Waskow, *From Race Riot to Sit-In,* Garden City, N.Y.: Doubleday and Co., 1967.

V. Police Violence

Michael Baker, et al., *Police on Campus: The Mass Police Action at Columbia University, Spring 1968,* New York: New York Civil Liberties Union, 1969.

George Berkley, *The Democratic Policeman,* Boston: Beacon Press, 1969.

Crisis at Columbia, New York: Vintage Books, 1968.

John Darnton, "Color Line a Key Police Problem," *New York Times* (September 28, 1969), pp. 1, 69.

Dissent and Disorder: A Report of the Citizens of Chicago on the April 27 Peace Parade, Chicago (August 1, 1968).

Edgar Z. Friedenberg, "A Violent Country," *New York Review of Books* (October 20, 1966), pp. 3–5.

John Hersey, *The Algiers Motel Incident,* New York: Bantam Books, 1968.

William Bradford Huie, *Three Lives for Mississippi,* New York: Trident Press, 1965.

Gene Marine, *The Black Panthers,* New York: Signet Books, 1969.

National Commission on the Causes and Prevention of Violence, *Rights in Conflict: The Chicago Police Riot,* New York: New American Library, 1968.

President's Commission on Law Enforcement and Administration of Justice, *The Challenge of Crime in A Free Society,* Washington: Government Printing Office, 1967.

Albert J. Reiss, Jr., "Police Brutality—Answers to Key Questions," *Transaction* (July-August, 1968), pp. 10–19.

Report of the National Advisory Commission on Civil Disorders, New York: Bantam Books, 1968.

Bobby Seale, *Seize the Time,* New York: Random House, 1970.

VI. Cultural Supports for Violence

Joe Flaherty, "The Hawks in May: A Day to Remember," *The Village Voice* (May 18, 1967), pp. 1, ff.

Winthrop Griffith, "People's Park—270′ × 450′ of Confrontation," *New York Times Magazine* (June 29, 1969), pp. 5, ff.

Otto N. Larsen (ed.), *Violence and the Mass Media,* New York: Harper and Row, 1968.

National Commission on the Causes and Prevention of Violence,

Firearms and Violence in American Life, Washington: Government Printing Office, 1969.

———, *To Establish Justice, To Insure Domestic Tranquility,* Washington: Government Printing Office, 1969.

———, *Violence and the Media,* Washington: Government Printing Office, 1969.

"Special Report From Berkeley," *Ramparts* (August 1969), pp. 34–59.

Fredric Wertham, *A Sign for Cain: An Exploration of Human Violence,* New York: Macmillan, 1966.

———, *Seduction of the Innocent,* New York: Holt, Rinehart and Winston, 1954.

Sheldon Wolin and John Schaar, "Berkeley: The Battle of the People's Park," *New York Review of Books* (June 19, 1969), pp. 24–31.

VII. The Future of Violence in America

William O. Douglas, *Points of Rebellion,* New York: Random House, 1970.

Geoffrey Gorer, "Man Has No Killer Instinct," *New York Times Magazine* (November 27, 1966), p. 47, ff.

Philip Green, "Can It Happen Here? Is It Already Happening," *New York Times Magazine* (September 20, 1970), pp. 30–31, ff.

National Commission on the Causes and Prevention of Violence, *To Establish Justice, To Insure Domestic Tranquility,* Washington: Government Printing Office, 1969.

Charles A. Reich, *The Greening of America,* New York: Random House, 1970.

Richard Rogin, "Joe Kelly Has Reached His Boiling Point," *New York Times Magazine* (June 28, 1970), pp. 12–24.

Theodore Roszak, *The Making of a Counter Culture,* Garden City, N.Y.: Doubleday and Co., 1969.

Bibliography

Abrahamsen, David, *Our Violent Society,* New York: Funk and Wagnalls, 1969.

Adamic, Louis, *Dynamite: The Story of Class Violence in America,* New York: Harper and Brothers, 1931.

Alex, Nicholas, *Black in Blue: A Study of the Negro Policeman,* New York: Appleton-Century-Crofts, 1969.

Anderson, Walt (ed.), *The Age of Protest,* Pacific Palisades, Calif.: Goodyear Publishing Co., 1969.

Andrist, Ralph K., *The Long Death: The Last Days of the Plains Indians,* New York: The Macmillan Co., 1964.

Annals of the American Academy of Political and Social Science, "Patterns of Violence," Special Issue, March, 1966.

Aptheker, Herbert, *American Negro Slave Revolts,* New York: Columbia University Press, 1943.

Ardrey, Robert, *African Genesis,* New York: Dell Publishing Co., 1967.

————, *The Territorial Imperative,* New York: Atheneum Publishers, 1966.

Arendt, Hannah, *On Violence,* New York: Harcourt, Brace and World, 1970.

Ashmore, Harry and William C. Baggs, *Mission to Hanoi,* New York: G. Putnam's Sons, 1968.

Avron, Jerry, *Up Against the Ivy Wall,* New York: Atheneum Publishers, 1968.

Baker, Michael, *et al., Police on Campus: The Mass Police Action At Columbia University, Spring 1968,* New York: New York Civil Liberties Union, 1969.

Bedau, Hugo A. (ed.), *The Death Penalty in America: An Anthology,* Garden City, N.Y.: Doubleday and Co., 1967.

Benedict, Ruth, *Patterns of Culture,* Boston: Houghton Mifflin Co., 1934.

Bennett, Lerone, Jr., *Before the Mayflower: A History of the Negro in America, 1619–1964,* Chicago: Johnson Publishing Co., 1964.

Berkley, George, *The Democratic Policeman,* Boston: Beacon Press, 1969.

Berkowitz, Leonard, *Aggression: A Social Psychological Analysis,* New York: McGraw-Hill, Inc., 1962.

Bienen, Henry, *Violence and Social Change,* Chicago: University of Chicago Press, 1968.

Billington, Ray A., *Westward Expansion,* New York: The Macmillan Co. 1960.

Bohannan, Paul (ed.), *African Homicide and Suicide,* Princeton, N.J.: Princeton University Press, 1960.

Bondurant, Joan V., *Conquest of Violence: The Ghandian Philosophy of Conflict,* Berkeley: University of California Press, 1967.

Bosworth, Allan R., *America's Concentration Camps,* New York: W. W. Norton Co., 1967.

Botkin, B.A., *Lay My Burden Down,* Chicago: University of Chicago Press, 1945.

Brandon, William, *The American Heritage Book of Indians,* New York: Dell Publishing Co., 1964.

Brinton, Crane, *The Anatomy of Revolution,* New York: Vintage Books, 1955.

Broehl, Wayne G., Jr., *The Molly Maguires,* Cambridge, Mass.: Harvard University Press, 1964.

Brown, H. Rap, *Die Nigger Die!* New York: The Dial Press, 1969.

Browne, Malcolm W., *The New Face of War,* Indianapolis and New York: Bobbs-Merrill Co., 1968.

Bruce, Robert V., *1877: Year of Violence,* Indianapolis and New York: Bobbs-Merrill Co., 1959.

Burchett, Wilfred, *Vietnam North,* New York: International Publishers, 1966.

Caffi, Andrea, *A Critique of Violence,* Indianapolis and New York: Bobbs-Merrill Co., 1969.

Carmichael, Stokely and Charles Hamilton, *Black Power: The Politics of Liberation in America,* New York: Vintage Books, 1967.

Cash, Wilbur J., *The Mind of the South,* New York: Alfred A. Knopf, Inc., 1941.

Chalmers, David M., *Hooded Americanism: The First Century of the Ku Klux Klan, 1865–1965,* Garden City, N.Y.: Doubleday and Co., 1965.

Chevigny, Paul, *Police Power: Police Abuses in New York City,* New York: Vintage Books, 1969.

Chicago Commission on Race Relations, *The Negro in Chicago,* Chicago: University of Chicago Press, 1922.

Collier, John, *Indians of the Americas,* New York: New American Library, 1947.

Connery, Robert H. (ed.), *Urban Riots,* New York: Vintage Books, 1969.

Conot, Robert, *Rivers of Blood, Years of Darkness,* New York: Bantam Books, 1967.

Cressey, Donald R., *Theft of the Nation: The Structure of Organized Crime in America,* New York: Harper and Row, Publishers, 1969.

Crisis at Columbia: Report of the Fact-Finding Commission Appointed to Investigate the Disturbances at Columbia University in April and May 1968, New York: Vintage Books, 1968.

Cutler, James E., *Lynch-Law: An Investigation into the History of Lynching in the United States,* New York: Longmans, Green Co., 1905.

Demaris, Ovid, *America the Violent,* New York: Cowles Book Co., 1970.

Dollard, John, *Caste and Class in a Southern Town,* Garden City, N.Y.: Doubleday and Co., 1949.

Donovan, James A., *Militarism, U.S.A.,* New York: Scribners, 1970.

Douglas, William O., *Points of Rebellion,* New York: Random House, 1970.

DuBois, W. E. B., *Black Reconstruction in America—1860–1880,* New York: Harcourt Brace and Co., 1935.

Duncan, Donald, *The New Legions,* New York: Random House, 1967.

Ellul, Jacques, *Violence,* New York: The Seabury Press, 1969.

Endleman, Shalom (ed.), *Violence in the Streets,* Chicago: Quadrangle Books, 1968.

Epstein, Jason, *The Great Conspiracy Trial,* New York: Random House, 1970.

Esposito, Vincent J. (ed.), *The West Point Atlas of American Wars,* New York: Frederick A. Praeger, 1959.

Fanon, Frantz, *The Wretched of the Earth,* New York: Grove Press, 1963.

Federal Bureau of Investigation, *Uniform Crime Reports,* Washington, Government Printing Office, 1969.

Foreman, Grant, *Indian Removal,* Norman, Okla.: University of Oklahoma Press, 1932.

Frank, Jerome, *Sanity and Survival: Psychological Aspects of War and Peace,* New York: Random House, 1968.

Franklin, John Hope, *From Slavery to Freedom,* New York: Alfred A. Knopf, 1948.

————, *The Militant South,* Boston: Beacon Press, 1964.

Fried, Morton, *et al., War: The Anthropology of Armed Conflict and Aggression,* New York: Museum of Natural History Press, 1968.

Fulbright, J. William, *The Arrogance of Power,* New York: Vintage Books, 1966.

Gerassi, John, *North Vietnam: A Documentary,* Indianapolis and New York: Bobbs-Merrill Co., 1968.

Ginzburg, Ralph, *100 Years of Lynchings,* New York: Lancer Books, 1962.

Gregg, Richard B., *The Power of Nonviolence,* New York: Schocken Books, 1966.

Grier, William H. and Price Cobbs, *Black Rage,* New York: Basic Books, 1968.

Grimshaw, Allen D. (ed.), *Racial Violence in the United States,* Chicago: Aldine Publishing Co., 1969.

Gurr, Ted Robert, *Why Men Rebel,* Princeton, N.J.: Princeton University Press, 1969.

Hagen, William T., *American Indians,* Chicago: University of Chicago Press, 1961.

Hammer, Richard, *One Morning in the War,* New York: Coward-McCann, 1970.

Harvey, Frank, *Air War—Vietnam,* New York: Bantam Books, 1967.

Hayden, Tom, *Rebellion in Newark,* New York: Vintage Books, 1967.

Heaps, Willard A., *Riots, U.S.A.: 1765–1965,* New York: The Seabury Press, 1966.

Helfer, Ray E., and Henry Kempe (eds.), *The Battered Child,* Chicago: University of Chicago Press, 1968.

Henry, Jules, *Culture Against Man,* New York: Random House, 1963.

Hersey, John, *The Algiers Motel Incident,* New York: Bantam Books, 1968.

Hersh, Seymour, *My Lai 4: A Report on the Massacre and its Aftermath,* New York: Random House, 1970.

Hobsbawm, Eric J., *Social Bandits and Primitive Rebels,* Glencoe, Ill.: The Free Press, 1959.

Hofstadter, Richard and Michael Wallace (eds.), *American Violence: A Documentary History,* New York: Alfred A. Knopf, 1970.

Hoig, Stan, *The Sand Creek Massacre,* Norman, Okla., University of Oklahoma Press, 1961.

Horsburgh, H. J. N., *Nonviolence and Aggression: A Study of Ghandi's Moral Equivalent of War,* New York: Oxford University Press, 1968.

Huie, William Bradford, *Three Lives for Mississippi,* New York: Trident Press, 1965.

Hunt, George T., *The Wars of the Iroquois,* Madison: University of Wisconsin Press, 1940.

In the Name of America, New York: Clergy and Laymen Concerned About Vietnam, 1968.

Jackson, Helen Hunt, *A Century of Dishonor,* New York: Harper and Brothers, 1881.

Jensen, Vernon H., *Heritage of Conflict,* Ithaca, N.Y.: Cornell Univ. Press, 1950.

Jones, Howard M., *Violence and Reason,* New York: Atheneum Publishers, 1969.

Josephy, Alvin, Jr., *The Indian Heritage of America,* New York: Alfred A. Knopf, 1968.

Kenniston, Kenneth, *Young Radicals: Notes on Committed Youth,* New York: Harcourt, Brace and World, 1968.

Knight, Oliver, *Following Indian Wars,* Norman, Okla.: University of Oklahoma Press, 1960.

Knoebl, Victor, *Victor Charlie,* New York: Frederick Praeger Publishers, 1967.

Lane, Mark, *Conversations With Americans,* New York: Simon and Schuster, 1970.

Larsen, Otto N. (ed.), *Violence and the Mass Media,* New York: Harper and Row, 1968.

Leckie, Robert, *The Wars of America,* New York: Harper and Row, 1968.

Lee, Alfred McClung and Norman D. Humphrey, *Race Riot,* New York: The Dryden Press, 1943.

Leiden, Carl and Karl M. Schmitt (eds.), *The Politics of Violence,* Englewood Cliffs, N.J.: Prentice-Hall, Inc., 1968.

Lens, Sidney, *The Military Industrial Complex,* Philadelphia: Pilgrim Press, 1970.

Lewis, Anthony, *Portrait of a Decade: The Second American Revolution,* New York: Random House, 1964.

Leyburn, James G., *Frontier Folkways,* New Haven, Conn.: Yale University Press, 1935.

Lorenz, Konrad, *On Aggression,* New York: Harcourt, Brace and World, 1966.

Lowie, Robert, *Indians of the Plains,* Garden City, N.Y.: Doubleday and Co., 1963.

Lynchings and What They Mean, Atlanta, Ga.: Southern Commission on the Study of Lynching, 1931.

Mailer, Norman, *Armies of the Night,* New York: New American Library, 1968.

Marine, Gene, *The Black Panthers,* New York: Signet Books, 1969.

McCague, James, *The Second Rebellion: The Story of the New York City Draft Riots of 1863,* New York: The Dial Press, 1968.

McCarthy, Mary, *Vietnam,* New York: Harcourt, Brace and World, 1967.

Mead, Margaret (ed.), *Cooperation and Competition Among Primitive Peoples,* New York: McGraw-Hill Book Co., 1937.

Mellman, Seymour, *Pentagon Capitalism,* New York: McGraw-Hill Book Co., 1970.

Momboisse, Raymond, *Riots, Revolts and Insurrections,* Springfield, Ill.: C. C. Thomas, 1967.

Montagu, M. F. Ashley (ed.), *Man and Aggression,* New York: Oxford University Press, 1968.

Morris, Desmond, *The Naked Ape: A Zoologist's Study of the Human Animal,* New York: McGraw-Hill Book Co., 1968.

National Commission on the Causes and Prevention of Violence, *Violence in America: Historical and Comparative Perspectives*

(Vol. 1), Washington: Government Printing Office, 1969.

———, *Violence in America: Historical and Comparative Perspectives* (Vol. 2), Washington: Government Printing Office, 1969.

———, *The Politics of Protest: Violent Aspects of Protest and Confrontation* (Vol. 3), Washington: Government Printing Office, 1969.

———, *Rights in Concord: The Response to the Counter-Inaugural Protest Activities in Washington, D.C.,* January 18–20, 1969 (Vol. 4), Washington: Government Printing Office, 1969.

———, *Shoot-Out in Cleveland: Black Militants and the Police, July 23, 1968* (Vol. 5), Washington: Government Printing Office, 1969.

———, *Shut It Down! A College in Crisis: San Francisco State College, October 1968–April 1969* (Vol. 6), Washington: Government Printing Office, 1969.

———, *Firearms and Violence in American Life* (Vol. 7), Washington: Government Printing Office, 1969.

———, *Assassination and Political Violence* (Vol. 8), Washington: Government Printing Office, 1969.

———, *Violence and the Media* (Vol. 9), Washington: Government Printing Office, 1969.

———, *Law and Order Reconsidered* (Vol. 10), Washington: Government Printing Office, 1969.

———, *To Establish Justice, To Insure Domestic Tranquility* (Final Report), Washington: Government Printing Office, 1969.

———, *Rights in Conflict: The Chicago Police Riot,* New York: New American Library, 1968.

Neihardt, John G., *Black Elk Speaks,* Lincoln, Neb.: University of Nebraska Press, 1961.

Nieburg, H. L., *Political Violence: The Behavioral Process,* New York: St. Martin's Press, 1969.

Parkman, Francis, *The Conspiracy of Pontiac and the Indian War,* Boston: Little, Brown and Co., 1879.

Peckerell, James H., *Vietnam in the Mud,* Indianapolis and New York: Bobbs-Merrill Co., 1966.

Peckham, Howard H., *Pontiac and the Indian Uprising,* Chicago: University of Chicago Press, 1947.

Pinkney, Alphonso, *Black Americans,* Englewood Cliffs, N.J.: Prentice Hall, 1969.

President's Commission on Law Enforcement and the Administration of Justice, *The Challenge of Crime in A Free Society,* Washington: Government Printing Office, 1967.

Proxmire, William, *Report from Wasteland: America's Military Industrial Complex,* New York: Frederick Praeger Publishers, 1970.

Raper, Arthur F., *The Tragedy of Lynching,* Chapel Hill: University of North Carolina Press, 1933.

Reich, Charles A., *The Greening of America,* New York: Random House, 1970.

Report of the National Advisory Commission on Civil Disorders, New York: Bantam Books, 1968.

Rose, Thomas (ed.), *Violence in America: A Historical and Contemporary Reader,* New York: Random House, 1969.

Roszak, Theodore, *The Making of A Counter Culture: Reflections on the Technocratic Society and its Youthful Opposition,* Garden City, N.Y.: Doubleday and Co., 1969.

Rubenstein, Richard E., *Rebels in Eden: Mass Political Violence in the United States,* Boston: Little, Brown and Co., 1969.

Rudwick, Elliott M., *Race Riot at East St. Louis, July 2, 1917,* Cleveland: World Publishing Co., 1966.

Russell, Bertrand, *War Crimes in Vietnam,* New York: Monthly Review Press, 1967.

Salisbury, Harrison, *Behind the Lines—Hanoi,* New York: Harper and Row, 1967.

Sandoz, Mari, *Cheyenne Autumn,* New York: Avon Books, 1964.

Scheer, Robert (ed.), *Eldridge Cleaver: Post Prison Writings and Speeches,* New York: Random House, 1969.

Schell, Jonathan, *The Village of Ben Suc,* New York: Alfred A. Knopf, 1967.

Schlesinger, Arthur, Jr., *Violence: America in the Sixties,* New York: New American Library, 1968.
Schramm, Melvin, Jack Lyle and Edwin B. Parker, *Television in the Lives of Our Children,* Stanford, Calif.: Stanford University Press, 1961.
Seale, Bobby, *Seize the Time: The Story of the Black Panther Party and Huey P. Newton,* New York: Random House, 1970.
Segal, Ronald, *The Race War,* New York: The Viking Press, 1967.
Sellin, Thorsten (ed.), *Capital Punishment,* New York: Harper and Row, 1967.
Shogan, Robert and Tom Craig, *The Detroit Riot,* Philadelphia: Chilton Books, 1964.
Sloan, Irving J., *Our Violent Past,* New York: Random House, 1970.
Sorel, Georges, *Reflections on Violence,* New York: The Free Press, 1950.
Spock, Benjamin and Mitchell Zimmerman, *Dr. Spock on Vietnam,* New York: Dell Publishing Co., 1968.
Stampp, Kenneth, *The Peculiar Institution,* New York: Vintage Books, 1956.
Steel, Ronald, *Pax Americana,* New York: The Viking Press, 1967.
Storr, Anthony, *Human Aggression,* New York: Atheneum Publishers, 1968.
Taft, Philip, *Organized Labor in American History,* New York: Harper and Row Publishers, 1964.
Taylor, Telford, *Nuremberg and Vietnam: An American Tragedy,* Chicago: Quadrangle Books, 1970.
Toch, Hans, *The Social Psychology of Social Movements,* Indianapolis and New York: Bobbs-Merrill Co., 1965.
————, *Violent Men,* Chicago: Aldine Publishing Co., 1969.
Turnbull, Colin M., *The Forest People: A Study of the Pygmies of the Congo,* New York: Simon and Schuster, 1961.
Underhill, Ruth M., *Red Man's America: A History of Indians*

in the United States, Chicago: University of Chicago Press, 1953.

Vickers, George (ed.), *Dialogue On Violence,* Indianapolis and New York: Bobbs-Merrill Co., 1968.

Wakefield, Dan, *Supernation at Peace and War,* Boston: Little, Brown and Co., 1968.

Waskow, Arthur I., *From Race Riot to Sit-In,* Garden City, N.Y.: Doubleday and Co., 1967.

Wineberg, Arthur and Lila, *Instead of Violence: Writings by the Great Advocates of Peace and Nonviolence Throughout History,* Boston: Beacon Press, 1963.

Wertham, Frederic, *A Sign for Cain: An Exploration of Human Violence,* New York: The Macmillan Co., 1966.

————, *Seduction of the Innocent,* New York: Holt, Rinehart and Winston, 1954.

West, George P., *Report on the Colorado Strike,* Washington: Commission on Industrial Relations, 1915.

White, Walter, *Rope and Faggot: A Biography of Judge Lynch,* New York: Alfred A. Knopf, Inc., 1929.

Wolfgang, Marvin E., *Patterns of Criminal Homicide,* Philadelphia: University of Pennsylvania Press, 1958.

————, (ed.), *Studies in Homicide,* New York: Harper and Row Publishers, 1967.

Williams, Robert F., *Negroes With Guns,* New York: Murzani and Munsell Publishers, 1962.

Wright, Quincy, *A Study of War,* Chicago: University of Chicago Press, 1942.

Yablonsky, Lewis, *The Violent Gang,* New York: The Macmillan Co., 1966.

Young, Leontine, *Wednesday's Children: A Study of Neglect and Abuse,* New York: McGraw-Hill Book Co., 1964.

Index

About the Author

ALPHONSO PINKNEY was born in 1930, and received his Ph.D. degree in sociology from Cornell University in 1961. He is Professor of Sociology at Hunter College of the City University of New York and from 1969 to 1971 was Visiting Professor of Sociology at the University of Chicago. Professor Pinkney is the author of *The Committed: White Activists in the Civil Rights Movement, Black Americans* and *Poverty and Politics in Harlem* (with Roger Woock). He is currently writing a book on black nationalism for Random House.